Love like GOD

Embracing Unconditional Love

Love like GOD

Embracing Unconditional Love

Caroline A. Shearer

Absolute Love Publishing

Love Like God

Embracing Unconditional Love

Published by

Absolute Love Publishing

USA

Cover design by Sarah Picciuto

Cover artwork © Jenny Speckels. Original abstract painting of an opening flower releasing white light. Inspired by the "Flower of Creation"

Cover headshot by Prabhakar Gopalan

ISBN:

978-0-9833017-0-7

Printed in the United States of America

For my parents

Contents

Introduction

We have been wired to love conditionally. It is time to free ourselves from these imposed constraints and return to our natural state of unconditional love.

Who Am I?

I am a student of unconditional love. Elements in my life have prompted me to explore the meaning of love and have brought me to a point where I see it, or its potential, everywhere. I am learning to remember my true nature, which is to love myself and others absolutely.

I could instantaneously allow this to happen – that possibility exists for all of us – but, like most, I have my own journey and make strides in my own time. For now, I embrace those moments of total freedom when I release my fears and my attachments and allow myself to feel the blissful love inside my heart.

As I began writing this introduction, the song, "Love is My Religion" by Ziggy Marley began playing. Before this moment, I'm not sure I'd ever even heard the song, but I feel like this is my message for you, dear readers. I had asked my angels for assistance finding the words to "help the most people, in the most ways" - and perhaps this theme is it.

In a sense, love *is* my religion. It is what defines my perception of the world. It is what brings me closer to an awareness of God and of all that is good in the world. If we all chose to define our thoughts and actions by the principle of love, what would result, but even more love?

I do believe all we need is love. And, we will get there through an awareness of the power and beauty of that love.

Who Should Read This Book?

Your mother, your sister, your wife, your daughter, your father, your brother, your husband, your son, your friend, your co-worker, your boss, your employee, your neighbor, the woman next to you on the subway, the man on the corner of the street, and YOU. This is a book for sharing and a book for giving. I believe we all can benefit from its message.

Why Do We Want to Love Unconditionally?

This is an important question. Why does it matter? Why is loving with conditions not enough?

It is because loving with conditions isn't really loving. It lacks purity, and it lacks a complete truth. It is, in its essence, not love. It can be affection or loyalty or devotion – and there may be moments when love shines through – but it is not love.

If we say to someone, "I will love you through all these situations – this great one, this bad one, this awful one – but, you know, there is this one thing … I can't love you through that." It's like saying, "You're almost worth it."

If we believe in God, we want to unconditionally love to follow His example. After all, who better to emulate than God?

We also want to offer unconditional love because that is what we most want to receive. Giving and receiving unconditional love work together, and we must allow both to attain either.

Unconditionally loving includes loving ourselves without expectation and without a need to be a certain way or do certain things. Many times, it is ourselves we claim to be "almost worth it." We can always choose to evolve our souls, but we can do so while *continuing to love ourselves absolutely.*

What Unconditional Love Means for Us

I find most people welcome the *idea* of unconditional love. People think it sounds wonderful and, of course, want to share in this magical kind of acceptance and love! "Let's go love, love, love!" they say. But, one moment away, they will admit that, really, it's just an ideal, we can't possibly love unconditionally in practice.

The human, earthly part of me would tend to agree. Right now, I don't think the vast majority of us are capable of unconditionally loving everyone, all of the time. However, my soul knows we *can*, and I choose to focus my thoughts and my heart on the ultimate reality of everyone loving unconditionally, in every moment. We will get there when *we all believe it is possible*.

Loving unconditionally is a return to our true nature, a place where fear does not exist. A place where our souls are truly blissful. Imagine that - bliss! All the time, in every moment!

It will begin with a *shift in our thoughts*.

These thought patterns will then begin to manifest more and more often in our *actions*.

These actions will fulfill us in inspiring ways and will *inspire others* to begin to think and act unconditionally.

Ultimately, *a critical mass will be reached* when we start to see spontaneous outpourings of unconditional love in the world.

Suddenly, as if by surprise, *the world will see itself through the lenses of unconditional love!*

"Love Like God" sets the stage for this change in consciousness. This book is the beginning.

The Contributors

Oh, my wonderful contributors! I feel such love for them and such respect for them, for sharing these very personal stories of learning unconditional love. These individuals all have graciously allowed me to share their journeys so that you, too, may be helped along and inspired to push forward in your journey of love.

Most of these participants are well known, but a few are everyday people, beautiful souls on a path toward a higher existence. I have taken great strides to keep the writing and presentation of the participants well-rounded and open and unconditionally loving. You will find a wide variety of individuals, in every field and from many backgrounds and beliefs – and I believe this enhances our ability to extend unconditional love *to all*.

When I began with only a concept – for people to share their stories of how they have learned unconditional love – I had no idea what to expect. We're not all writers. Not everyone grasps the concept of unconditional love. Would people understand what I wanted? Would I even get responses?

It's funny, but I brushed those thoughts aside with the image of a feather duster. "Hello! Now, goodbye! I've got things to do with my life!" I trusted. I never doubted myself, and I never doubted the book would happen. I always knew this book would be made real, and it would help the world.

So simple.

And, as I went through this process, my intention was affirmed constantly. Every perfect participant and story came to me. It was like opening a present every time another one approached me. Topics flowed to me gracefully and beautifully. More and more each day, I truly understood that this project was meant to happen and was meant to touch people's lives in a meaningful way. I know that we have exactly the right stories in this book.

It was with this project that I finally was able to put into practice my understanding of accepting the flow of the universe as my best course.

And what a blessing that has proven to be!

Once we choose goodness and make it a conscious decision, the smaller parts of that intention become easier. The universe helps us stay within the flow of what our soul desires.

I ask you to honor the humbleness of these individuals, that they were able to share their heartfelt stories with you in such a public way. Understand that writing about these experiences helped to crystallize in their own hearts and in their own minds what they have learned. It has been a growth experience for all of us. And I believe all readers will find a story, and likely more than one, that truly resonates with their heart.

We are prepared. We are on the path.

Unconditionally loving is an evolving process, and, even a year from now, we will be in a different place. But, now, right now, in this moment, this book reflects our consciousness. This book reflects our state of unconditionally loving.

This book is not the end-all, definitive book on unconditional love. It is a starting point. From one - many. As each of us evolves, so do many others.

Catch These Blocks Before They Grow

Sometimes when I mention unconditional love, people react defensively. One reason is a fear of losing control. They are complacent exerting conditions on those they love because it helps them feel they have a semblance of control. Releasing these conditions would create a situation, in their minds, where their carefully crafted worlds might spiral uncontrollably.

Solution: Recognizing that we do not control anyone but ourselves will release this illusion and allow us to embrace the natural flow of life.

People also resist unconditional love due to a misinterpretation of its meaning. They sometimes believe loving unconditionally means allowing others to treat them poorly, without any repercussions. Absolutely not! Sometimes our best path is to love someone from a distance. If someone is treating us in a way that doesn't reflect our divine soul, or if we are in a non-supportive environment - then it is part of loving ourselves to break free.

Solution: Setting boundaries for what we choose to have present in our lives will affirm unconditional love for ourselves.

We sometimes want to make ourselves right and the other person wrong. But, is that really ever the case? Perhaps that soul accepted the responsibility of making a "mistake" so we could learn from the situation. How many people in our lives do we have a tendency to blame, and how might they have helped us? Consider that our enemies and our victimizers may actually be our greatest saviors.

Solution: Recognizing each moment and each person as a gift toward the evolution of our souls will allow us to understand the lesson in all.

A Note about the Layout of "Love Like God"

Every time I began to segment this book, to divide it into topics, something held me back. And, as I looked into it, I realized that labels weren't working because each type of unconditional love flows into others. Learning unconditional love is not just about learning to love oneself, or learning to love others, or learning to love animals – it is all interrelated, as we are, as our universe is. To this end, I organized the stories alphabetically, and readers will enjoy finding nuggets of wisdom - sometimes in surprising places - along the way.

This includes, for example:

That everything from autism to Alzheimer's can be a gift, in stories like Portia Allen's and Lori La Bey's

How international peace can be achieved, through the example of Lisa Gibson

What every husband should know, according to former professional baseball player Jon Graves

Dealing with addictions, in our own lives and others', in stories by Crystal Dwyer, Roy Nelson, and Kristen Moeller

Why releasing blame creates freedom, according to Lorelei Shellist

The most valuable lesson medical students, nurses, and social workers can learn, by Dr. Joseph Shrand

Readers also will find my words of reflection and an affirmation with each story. Find what holds meaning to your heart, and read it over and over again, as you absorb the loving message into your soul. Feel the energy in the words. Feel your intention and the collective intention, and allow yourself to be enveloped in this flow of unconditional love.

My Philosophy
on Unconditional Love

It is our natural state to give and receive unconditional love.

What we crave most in the world is the conscious knowledge that we are unconditionally loved.

We are able to love unconditionally when we release fears and expectations.

God loves everyone unconditionally.

We erase perceived pain when we are in a state of unconditional love.

Loving ourselves unconditionally is essential for loving others unconditionally.

When we begin to love ourselves unconditionally, we see beautiful transformation in our lives.

I am love.

You are love.

Discovering Unconditional Love

Thoughts from Caroline

Which one of us hasn't been presented by God with a change in "our" plans? And, when it happens, how often is our first reaction one of blame – blame of others, ourselves, bad luck, life? When we choose to see these changes as corrections in our larger life path instead of reasons for blame, we can learn to see their value. What lessons do they bring? What attachment is it in our best interest to release? If we can trust that everything - every single thing in our lives – is present in order to help us, we can grow smoothly and quickly into the beautiful, unconditionally loving nature of our souls.

Affirmation

I am open to life's surprises and view them as opportunities to grow in love.

Portia Berry Allen

*entertainer, spokesperson, model, actress, and avid supporter of
the Autism Foundation*

What is love? Love is thoughtful, love is kind, love is family, and love is *everything*. How was I, Portia "Lady Rerun" Allen, taught unconditional love? Well, let's start at the beginning.

My father, Fred "Rerun" Berry, was a member of the famous dance troupe, "The Lockers," and the star of NBC's 1970s sitcom, "What's Happening!" My mother, Carlise Keeton, was a featured dancer for Soul Train from 1976 to 1978. Though their relationship was questioned by everyone, the two were best friends.

My father always said my mother treated him like a real person, and it was this that made him respect and love her, despite his trust issues. In turn, my mother spoke fondly of him and told stories that made me see him through her eyes. Together they taught me about love. Even though they never married, I always felt their love for each other and for me.

But, our situation was neither simple nor easy. My father's career took up most of his time and energy, and, as I grew up, I had to learn to look past the fact that he was unable to put much effort into his relationship with me. I realized that if I wanted a relationship with him, I would have to create it.

So, I did. I invested a great deal of love and energy into my relationship with my father. I did *more*, without anger or resentment. I knew that the solidity and strength of our relationship was due to the time and work I put into it, but I didn't let that change my love for him. I understood that his career did not give him the necessary time to devote to our relationship. I loved him anyway.

Thankfully, my mother encouraged me. Unlike many mothers, she never tried to stop me from pursuing a relationship with my father. There was no backbiting or animosity between them. Their friendship gave me the opportunity to pursue the type of relationship with my father that I wanted. And, he was grateful for it. He told me he was happy that I didn't give up on him or on our relationship - that everyone else gave up on him but I didn't. He was happy I had pursued the relationship.

Unfortunately, few others understood. I received a lot of flak for my efforts. People often told me, "He should not be doing that to you." I responded, "He is my father. I want a relationship with my father." To me, it was self-evident: If you want a relationship with someone, you work to establish one.

If people complained about their own fathers, I would ask, "What do you do to make things better? Why do you let your father's actions determine how you feel about him? Why do you turn away just because he doesn't do what you think he should do?" It was these principles that guided me.

Perhaps because of my unconventional parentage, I longed to be a conventional parent. I always knew I would be a mother, and I knew exactly how it would happen. I would fall in love, get married, and have beautiful children. I had a set plan, set goals, and I was determined to see them through! I had daydreams in which I would brag about my children and their accomplishments. Daydreams in which they did everything - from walking to talking to potty training and everything in between - right on time.

Was I in for a rude awakening! On March 3, 2007, the first of my twin sons was diagnosed with autism. In that moment, my entire world collapsed. As I sat at the table and heard the developmental pediatrician say, "Your son has autism," I was shocked. It felt like a big slap in the face.

There is a big difference in thinking you know something and *knowing* you know something. When you hear those words from a qualified person, it is the most devastating experience of your life. It was like someone telling me that I or my loved one was terminal. It had the same emotional backlash. I had to wonder if our lives would ever be normal again.

At first, I blamed myself. Was it something I did? Was it something I ate? Did I not take enough vitamins? No matter who you are, what education you have, what tax bracket you are in - when you first get that diagnosis, you blame yourself – especially if you are the mother because you carried the child. It was hard to convince myself that I didn't cause my son's autism. It took time for me to learn it was not my fault, that it was nobody's fault, that devastating things happen, and no one is to blame.

Then, there was, "Why? Why did it happen to me? To my child?" The denial and the blame were even worse in my case because it delayed my recognition of autistic symptoms in my other child. He was diagnosed a year later, and that guilt almost suffocated me.

When I arrived at the point where I forgave myself, the healing started. That is when I focused: Let's get the therapy; let's get intervention!

Who knew this experience was going to change the way I love, the way I think of love, and how I recognize real, unconditional love? My twins are the most loving boys in the world, and every day I am amazed they are mine. Even though one is non-verbal and the other is verbal with many speech issues, they have taught me the true meaning of unconditional love in a way I never thought possible. They have taught me that love is simple and can be communicated in the simplest of ways.

When you have a challenging situation and are able to bring yourself out of that situation and transform it into positivity and light, there is a reason why. There is a reason why my children were born with autism. There is a lesson for me in this, and there is a lesson for everyone around me.

I now appreciate the little things in life, and my kids are learning to love because of the love I put into what I do with them every day. I'm always praising them. I'm always telling them that I love them and that I adore them. I constantly reiterate my love and affection for them, without condition, without a "*because....*" There is so much repetition with kids – I need especially to repeat that I love them!

Love makes things better. It fills life with joy. Love makes you want to do everything you do more often and better. I don't get up in the morning and go through the learning rituals with my children because I have to or because I am their mother. I do it for the love of it. I do it because I *want* to do it. What you put in is what you get out!

Recently, an awe-inspiring moment proved that to me. My son came home from school and handed me an envelope that said, "Student of the Month." I was floored! I looked at my son and pulled him close. My heart grew to the size of a blimp. It almost burst out of my chest! I was so proud of him!

I never thought I would hear those type of words associated with one of my kids. When children are diagnosed with autism, you give up the idea that you are going to hear academic praise. You never think you are going to be able to celebrate the achievements other children would celebrate. I was full of joy and love.

Later, I found out he was at grade level academically. It was mind-boggling to me! He went from being nonverbal and barely able to count on his fingers to being grade level in kindergarten at the age of five. It shows what unconditional love and determination can accomplish. I may not have all the technical skills necessary for his education, but I have the love and I have the determination to get the therapy he needs or to teach myself how to provide the therapy if I have no other resource.

Love becomes stagnant when conditions are placed on it. My child's rise to meet his challenges is an example of what unconditional love can do for a child, for a family, for a mother. When it is truly unconditional, there are no boundaries love can't cross!

We cannot offer others what we cannot offer ourselves, and I would not be able to offer unconditional love to my children if I hadn't gone through my most difficult lesson in unconditional love - learning to love myself. I have a body size and shape that has made me a target of bullies and people who thought the best way for me to be socially acceptable was not to eat at all!

And, I was my own worst enemy. I felt rejected by society, and I hated myself so much that I entered a dark time that could have ended badly. Learning to love myself, my true self, was one of the hardest tasks I have ever had to face. I was blessed to have real friends who loved me for me, and who helped me crawl out of the hole I made for myself. Even through my other lessons, I had to knock down the conditions I had built against my own self-love.

Thankfully, I am now deeply and passionately in love with myself, and no one can change or take away that love! It is real, it is strong, and it is abiding! It is here for me, and it is here to share with all those whose lives I am blessed to touch. Our greatest gift, our greatest blessing is love, true love, a love without conditions!

Thoughts from Caroline

Betrayal. Loss of trust. Trauma of the heart. These are some of the most devastating emotions we can experience. Our world crumbles, and we feel that all we have believed to be true was merely an illusion. These are moments where we face decisions crucial to our growth: Do we allow it to continue? Do we walk away? Or do we forgive or change? It is in that choice that we cement our belief in unconditional love because each path provides growth toward love – for ourselves and for the other.

Affirmation

Loving myself unconditionally will heal my relationships with others.

K.L. Belvin

author of "From Gigolo to Jesus" and "A Man in Transition" and co-founder of Bravin Publishing, LLC

Tiffany Braxton Belvin

Miss New York Plus America 2010, Creative Director for Bravin Publishing, LLC, and author

Tiffany was different. Whereas most women seemed concerned with their outward appearance, Tiffany was not. While her beauty was undeniable, she also looked like she was homeless. When we met, I was 28 years old, in college, and arrogant. I judged women by what they wore and how they styled their hair, and I connected those feelings to insensitive ideas.

After I met Tiffany, I asked her why she wore the clothes she wore. She said she owned a home, and all her money went to her mortgage. I didn't believe her. I was so used to not telling the truth that I thought everyone was as deceitful as I was. I even waited until our first date to tell Tiffany I was married. I was sure I had secured my way in, but I was sadly mistaken. Her values were on a totally different level than her wardrobe, and I was sacked before I even got to play the game. It took another five years before I got a shot at stardom in Tiffany's life.

When I met KL, I was 19 years old and thought the world should and did revolve around me. I was in my third year of college, had two jobs, and owned a house. I was impressed this older gentleman, who I found very handsome, eloquent, and charismatic, took an interest in me. I wouldn't give him the time of day, though, because KL was also obnoxious, obscenely vain, and married. After our first date, he told me he had a wife and children, as if he was certain it wouldn't be an obstacle because he was accustomed to women who overlooked it.

Unlike his other women, I completely shut down. I had been through my share of good and bad relationships, and, by that point, I was firm on what I wouldn't tolerate. Married men were at the top of the list. It would take five years and a pending divorce before he could even try to change my mind.

When Tiffany and I eventually entered a relationship together, I continued to live the lifestyle of my first marriage, and infidelity was a regular occurrence. But, one fateful day, Tiff turned to me and asked, "How long have you been cheating on me?" I was shocked, but, as a trained cheater, I remained calm. I thought she didn't have any evidence. But, I soon learned, when an intelligent woman has you caught, there is no way out.

I felt lower than a man could feel. Tiff had always been honest and caring. In the past, when I was caught doing something, I didn't worry - I would simply pack up and move on. This time was different. Tiffany was special. She was the woman I wanted to spend my life with, the woman I wanted to marry, and I loved being with her. I had just ripped her heart from her chest, and, in return, I had hurt myself. I had never realized how devastating such emotions were.

The life of a cheater is one of utter confusion. On one hand, you're happily living foul, and, on the other hand, you're trying the best you can to make your significant other happy. Light and dark cannot occupy the same existence, and I had been trying to make a scientific impossibility work. As she walked away, I had no idea how to fix what I'd done. Yet, I knew in my heart that a life without her was no longer an option.

When I found out KL had been with other women, it was the most disappointing moment in our relationship. We had discussed my feelings on infidelity many times, and I had shared my theory that there were enough women who didn't mind man-sharing that he should respect me not wanting to participate. I gave him the option to let me know if at any time he felt he could not be faithful. I told him I would graciously walk away.

I had given him so much more credit than he deserved at the time. It hurt that he was unfaithful, but it hurt more that he allowed other women to believe they were better than me and that I wasn't fulfilling my responsibilities in the relationship. I was hurt that, in his mistresses' minds, he had reduced my place in his life to one that deserved so little respect, from them and from him.

However, each time I pulled a skeleton out of his closet, it brought me closer to the reasons why he cheated. I realized his actions had nothing to do with the other women in his life and nothing to do with me. He was suffering from his own insecurities, and the multitude of other women fueled his wavering self-esteem. I realized it wasn't my battle to fight. Instead, I prayed for him to find peace within himself, and I prayed to find my own peace in letting him go, if that was what I needed to do. After all, I did love him and wanted him to be happy, and it was obvious he wasn't.

After much prayer, I decided to give KL a choice. I told him I was willing to stick by him and work it out, if he promised it would never happen again. It was up to him whether to have a monogamous relationship with me - someone who was willing to go the distance with him - or to continue his previous behavior of jumping from one woman to another. He understood I was serious and that I was prepared to accept whatever choice he made. I knew when I made my stand that, although KL loved me, he may not be able to appreciate being loved by me. I was prepared to walk away.

Tiff ultimately forgave me, and there isn't a day that goes by that I'm not thankful for her forgiveness. Together we moved past the insurrections to build a fantastic union, and she has brought so much happiness into my life. Many couples don't know how to forgive and forget. Our faith requires us to do exactly that for each other. We use our faith to lay the foundation for our marriage.

Since Tiff's decision to forgive me and our joint decision to put the cheating behind us, we have experienced what many couples can only dream of - true happiness. All healing needs a source from which to spring, and Tiffany's commitment to faith and her forgiveness of my actions served as the well from which we drew the necessary strength. When I saw the way Tiff dealt with the man I was, how compassionate, loving, caring, intelligent, and strong-willed she was, I knew I wanted to move forward with our relationship and marry her.

I had been previously married for eight years, and reconnecting with Tiff was a breath of fresh air. When you have done something the wrong way, and a person comes into your life with new ideas, your heart can be instantly healed. Back in college, I had told a friend she was "my diamond in the rough" and that someday she would be mine. Once we reconnected, I had a feeling there was more between us than "just a relationship." Over our years of dating, we moved closer to becoming the married couple neither one of us had seen in our younger years with our own parents. She was truly what I wanted in a wife.

When KL told me he wanted me to be his wife, I had no doubts as to whether I would accept him as my husband. He told me he wanted me to give him my heart because he was going to make me the happiest woman in the world. And, he has. Like many other women, I wanted to love and to be loved, but I also wanted someone who would appreciate me loving him and who could appreciate loving me. KL has made it easy to love him without reservation. His sensitivity, attentiveness, nurturance, and protectiveness make me feel safe. Even as an extremely independent person, I am not afraid of losing control. KL goes above and beyond to make me feel secure in our relationship in every way.

Our marriage is what many think a good marriage should be. We love being married, and we believe that it is our spiritual foundation that keeps our marriage so strong. Our marriage is filled with the substances needed to have pure happiness. It is our belief that there isn't anything that can block true love, but you have to be willing to work at it and be committed to the idea of the relationship. For us, our faith is at the center of our commitment. If we begin from there, we can and will only grow closer.

Thoughts from Caroline

Sometimes we are provided an opportunity not only to forgive, but to release – our pain, our resentment, our perceived injustice. It is important in these times to realize that it is our choice. God provides us free will so we can make the best decision we are able to make, in that moment. At times, we surprise even ourselves when we take giant leaps forward in our soul's evolution and act more loving than we ever imagined we could. In these moments, unconditional love is a tangible presence and a healer of all.

Affirmation

" *Love overcomes all.* "

I remember it was a Wednesday night, and I was out fishing with my four-year-old son and a friend. I received a call on my cell phone, but I didn't answer it. After a little while, I put down my fishing pole and went to see who had called. It was my wife. She had left a message that said she needed me to be home by eight because a mentor of mine, Richard Mull, was going to be there. I was confused about why he would be coming over to my house. He had never been there before, and I could not figure out why he would be coming over that late. But, we packed up and headed home anyway.

I called Richard when I was about ten minutes from my house, and I could hardly speak. I asked him if Kara had cheated on me. He did not answer yes or no but instead asked me to wait until he got to my house so we could talk. I lost it. It was a mixture of trying to catch my breath and sobs. I was very aware that my son was in the backseat so I tried my best to keep it together, but I had a very difficult time. I told myself there was a different reason he was on his way over. I would get home, and it would be something else, and I would be so relieved. I told myself there was no way she could do that to me. Not my wife. Not Kara.

Somehow, I made it back to my house and pulled into the driveway. I felt numb. I could hardly stand as I let my son out of the car and followed him in to the house. Kara was inside on the couch, and as we entered, she took our son upstairs and put him and my daughter to bed. In the meantime, I walked over to the couch opposite of hers and sat down. I had a hooded sweatshirt on, and I pulled the hood up and over my face. I did not know what else to do. I felt void of everything. I felt like I had already lost everything. I just wanted her to come downstairs and give me the relief I desperately wanted.

It took about ten minutes before she came back downstairs. Instead of coming over to me, she sat back in the spot she was in when we got home. She was silent. There was fear on her face, and she looked torn. We sat in silence for a minute, and there was no way I wanted to ask the question that I had to ask. However, I knew that I needed to ask it so it came out like vomit. I did not even look at her, and my head was still under the hood when I asked with a shaky voice, "Who was it with?"

She came unglued. She immediately started to sob and wail, and as she caught her breath between sobs, she asked, "Can't we just wait until Richard gets here?"

My response was louder now and less shaky: "No! Who was it with?"

She continued to sob. "You know him," she said.

I didn't know if I had heard right. "What?" I asked.

She replied, "You know him."

I was lost in a world of disbelief and pain. My life was over. I had never known such pain. It felt like there was a jagged and rusty knife thrust inside me, ripping and tearing me apart. My world was crumbling around me, and there was nothing I could do to stop it. I wanted to vomit. I could not breathe, and my head was spinning. I was in shock. I just could not believe what she was telling me. I wanted to call her a liar, and tell her that I was not going to believe it.

I felt like I was in a movie. It did not feel real. This kind of thing happens to other people, not to me! I decided I needed a walk so I left the house and started down the street. As I walked, I had the urge to run and to never stop. If I could just run away, the pain would stay back there. I could start a new life. I did not have to stay with her - Jesus gives an exception for divorce. He said it is permissible if there is unfaithfulness.

As I pondered these things, I looked up and saw Richard's van as it came down the street. I stumbled over to the passenger side and fell in. I looked at him, and the emotion started to come. I began to sob, and I told him I did not want to go back there, that I did not have to stay. I repeated again that I did not have to stay. I was so broken.

He pulled into my driveway and talked to me until I was ready to go inside. I followed him inside and collapsed on the stairs. Kara was still in the same spot she had been in when I left. The moment she saw Richard, she lost it and began to apologize over and over.

I stood up and went to the bedroom and started to pack a bag. I planned to go to my parents to spend the night. Richard came in the room and talked to me again. He asked if I wanted to hear what God had to say. I said, *"No!"* Honestly, I was not interested in what God had to say at that point because I knew He was going to ask me to do something I really did not want to do.

After a couple of minutes, Richard left the bedroom and prayed with Kara. Alone in the bedroom, I didn't know what to do. After a while, Richard left, and Kara came into the bedroom, shaking and crying. I could no longer hold myself up so I dropped to the floor. Kara came over and collapsed in front of me. At that moment, I began to realize that I was not the same person I had been.

As I looked at my broken wife, I was overcome with compassion from God. As He filled me with mercy, I decided I was ready to listen. God told me to open my arms and embrace my wife. It took every ounce of my strength to open my arms to her. At first, I didn't think I could do it, but then God gave me even more of His strength and resolve. I opened my arms, and it was at that moment that God put us on the fast track to recovery. It was at that point I told her I chose to forgive her.

Kara looked up at me in disbelief. She was shocked by what I had said. She couldn't understand why I would forgive her. She told me she would do anything I asked. I looked at her a moment as God gave me another dose of grace, and I said, "I want you to forgive yourself."

Kara would later tell me she had never really understood the grace and unconditional love of God until that moment. There was a dark and intense battle for my soul that night. I shudder when I think about the different ways it could have gone.

I did leave that night and go to my parents' house. They were up when I got there, and we talked for a while. The next day, I went home, and my parents took the kids for the weekend. The next couple of days were a mixture of unbelievable pain and miraculous healing. The months that followed were just as interesting.

Kara and I are not the same people we used to be. Not by a long shot. Our relationship is not the same as it once was. This may sound unbelievable, but our marriage is so much better! We are both healed and being healed and continue to be made whole. It has been amazing. God has done so much for us since that Wednesday night!

I am not saying that it has been an easy road. There were numerous times when I was so down I did not think I could live anymore. I have been to the depths, and it's an ugly place. There were many times I wanted to just leave her, and a couple times I almost walked out of the door. I carried around so much heaviness. There were so many tears and an indescribable heartache.

But, God worked a miracle. God restored my marriage. Kara and I are still together, and we now have a more intimate relationship than we have ever had.

It took nine months for my heart to heal. Now, almost every time I have thoughts about that night, the emotional response that used to accompany them is dead. There is no pain, resentment, fear, blame, despair, hopelessness, bitterness, anger, or regret. God healed me.

"Love never fails." That's what the Bible says. But, many of us would say we have seen love fail time after time. This tragedy in my life caused me to examine love, and I came to realize that the Bible is right: Love never fails us. We fail love. Love is neither a feeling nor an emotion. Feelings and emotions are birthed by love. My wife may have failed me, but she failed love first. I have failed love so many times in my life; I cared only about myself for many years. Our lack of understanding prevented us from being saturated by love. It destroyed our ability to love each other.

The Bible says God is love. When this truth begins to penetrate our souls, we begin to see how empty we are and also how full we could be. Love is forgiveness, grace, and mercy. Love is total surrender and selflessness. Love is reconciliation and redemption. Love is God.

My wife and I were saved because we both began to finally understand what love is. And, that truth transformed us. As we walk today, we continue to grow in our understanding of love, and it continues to make us whole, individually and as a couple. It can be the same for you. God bless.

Thoughts from Caroline

Our souls follow their own unique paths. We honor our individual journeys by recognizing that we are not able to choose the actions of another soul. Sometimes our only option in a challenging situation is to send someone unconditional love. The often-unrecognized beauty in these situations, however, is that unconditional love is the greatest gift we can bestow on another. Whatever choices are ultimately made and whatever the outcome, unconditional love blesses the path.

Affirmation

Our individual journeys teach us love.

Love Like God

Chase Block

high school student and author of "Chasing Happiness: One Boy's Guide to Helping Other Kids Cope with Divorce, Parental Addictions and Death"

I was living a life of unconditional love long before I would learn what that meant.

From the time I was five, my beautiful, wonderful mom would get in dark moods when she was upset or depressed. She and I were always very, very close, and I was the one in the family who was around her the most. Dad was busy with work, and my two older brothers were at school. I took on the role of "family clown" to make her laugh. I'd also start to talk about happy family memories, and she'd slowly start to be her old self again.

We know now that she was in a deep depression, but, at the time, we didn't realize how serious it was. All I knew as a kid was that when Mom would start the slide down into that dark hole, she would get very quiet and wouldn't sleep. She'd start to repeat her words and talk in circles while she cleaned obsessively. I would laugh and try to make her see how ridiculous she was being; none of us knew how intense those demons were in her darkness.

At times, it was exhausting, and I wouldn't want to deal with it. But I learned early that sometimes love means pushing through it and trying to be there for her as much as I could. When I could make her happy and get her to start to laugh again, it was all worth it to me, even when I would have rather been doing my own stuff. I loved to spend time with her.

She and my dad always had a good relationship – he worked very hard to keep that door open – and he was also proud of the way I could usually help her get on top of her moods. He also wanted me to have time to do my own thing and just be a kid.

I never really discussed my mom's dark times with my friends because it wasn't any of their business. Besides, they all loved Mom, too. When I'd bring friends home with me, she was thrilled. She was happiest when the house was full of people, and she could cook for them and have great conversations with everyone. It was fun for all of us.

When it became apparent that Mom was heading downhill fast and abusing prescription medications, I made the tough decision to have a serious talk with her. I told her I couldn't see her again until she got help to beat her addiction.

My dad and I discussed it before I talked to Mom, and he said it was the right thing to do. I guess in a way it's the greatest kind of love – doing something that breaks your heart because you feel it's the only way to save someone's life. I was the one she loved most in the world, and I knew our connection was the only possible thing that might make her change her destructive ways. My reasoning was to push her to the bottom level and tell her I'd be waiting on the other side when she was well again. Whether she agreed to get help or not, it was going to be a tough battle. I went with tough love.

Instead of agreeing to go to rehab, she took her life two weeks later.

The more love you have for someone, the more his or her sudden death is tragic. It messes you up. The pain changes slowly over time, but you never really get over it. I wanted to share the story about her death in my book to help me cope with the sorrow. I also hoped that maybe my story could help other kids.

Relationships aren't as easy for me now. As you grow up, your mom is the one person you're supposed to trust the most. After she took her own life, I felt like I had been let down. Her death has made me more hesitant to let someone else in my heart.

I can't trust people right off the bat anymore. Once you've felt as let down as I did, you build up walls inside you to protect you from experiencing those feelings again. When you realize you don't know for sure what someone will do, it makes it hard to open up to anyone. But, at the same time, when you open up to someone, when you let down those walls, you get to experience unconditional love, which is like protection against vulnerability. Or being vulnerable in the best way.

I'm not saying I won't ever love someone unconditionally again. I hope I do, but it's harder now. Loving unconditionally is hard; it's the hardest thing you can do. But, it's definitely worth it. It teaches you maturity, loyalty, and important life lessons. It makes the word "love" mean something more than how most people use it. Most of all, it makes you stronger. You learn to love yourself better and to trust yourself more.

Thoughts from Caroline

The closest vision we have on earth to seeing pure, innocent, unconditional love is in the eyes of a child. Children are a reminder of who we can be and of who we really are. When we are blessed by the presence of children, we have an opportunity to connect with and experience unconditional love in a wondrous way. When we are blessed with the opportunity to raise children, we learn from their reflection of us, and we can reconnect with the pure, innocent part of our own hearts.

Affirmation

Children can be our greatest teachers on the path of love.

I grew up in a small town in Tennessee with stars in my eyes and big city dreams. I began reading fashion magazines as a kid, and I was sewing and making my own clothes by the time I turned eight. I was very fortunate to experience my dreams on a small scale in my hometown; I modeled in print ads throughout the southern region and did local commercials for car ads, groceries stores, and local television stations.

When I was eighteen, I landed a spokesmodel position with Eastman Kodak, and that was my quick claim to fame. I had a wonderful woman take me under her wings, Lynne Parks, who worked for Time Life in New York at the time and commuted back and forth from Greenville, Tennessee. She brought me to New York and helped me get more commercial print ad gigs. She also moved me in with Charlie Ryan's family at their home in Forest Hills, New York. He was a leading talent agent in New York.

My career was always the most important thing to me so the desire to start a family was the last thing on my mind for many years. I was very selfish and only thought of myself and my own wants and needs. My life was always about me and my next career move. I traveled the world working the circuit, taking one job after another, never really feeling ready to settle down or have a family.

But, one day, it happened.

I had known Rick, a national commercial developer and investor from Tennessee, for two years, and we were good friends. Then, one day, out of nowhere, it just clicked. We fell in love, and he became my best friend and my soul mate.

Joining his family, however, was a challenge. When we got together, Rick already had two children: Julia, a tall beauty of 24, and Chelsea, who was ten at the time. Her father and grandma had been raising her all by themselves. So, right out of the gate our life revolved around me being a mother.

Falling in love with a man who had a readymade family was one of the toughest things I've ever done. It has also been a blessing and one of the greatest gifts I've ever received. Both children have different mothers and completely different personalities so meeting them and establishing a relationship with each of them was a challenge.

Julia took center stage and first priority at the time that Rick and I became a couple. At almost six feet tall with legs to the moon and long, dark hair, Julia was a gorgeous and talented young woman, who had been prepped her entire life to become a beauty queen. She also had her sights set on becoming a recording artist. Her life was full of regiments and schedules.

Julia had just won the title of Miss West Virginia, and she was traveling West Virginia to fulfill her platform and title. She had a list of needs a mile long every time we turned around. And, there was Chelsea, just going with the flow, never really needing or wanting anything - an adorable, humble child.

We went to Atlantic City, full court press and entourage in tow, to support Julia's efforts to compete in the Miss America pageant. And, from there, we jumped straight into helping her with her endeavor to pursue a career in the music industry as a country music artist. We flew all around the country to watch her perform and spent countless hours helping her with wardrobe, image, and numerous labors of love to help her become successful.

Chelsea, who lives with us and who I have had the opportunity to raise as my own daughter, has stolen my heart, and I live and breathe for her and her happiness. I have spent the last eight years loving her, encouraging her, and helping her find herself and her passions. She has blossomed into a beautiful young woman.

Despite what I thought was my original career-minded track, my proudest moments in life have been about these two young women and their accomplishments. I love both of them as my very own and could not love them more, even if I had given birth to them and carried them in my womb for nine months. I want nothing other than to see them thrive and be happy and successful. My heart knows no boundaries or reservations with them. I look at them and my heart overflows with love and compassion.

I have had numerous challenges at times throughout the years, as I'm sure any parent experiences with their children. I get my feelings hurt sometimes, but I move on. My heart is open and full of love; it knows no boundaries. It overflows with happiness, pride and joy for these children. Through them, I have discovered the truly pure and selfless love of motherhood.

I came to the realization gradually that I had grown into the role of mothering these girls. Julia had been raised by her mother, and I had met her as an adult, but she and I both found we could gain from each other's presence in our lives. Chelsea had not been with her mother since a very young age, and, after I fell in love with her, I never hesitated to claim her for my own.

The blessing and opportunity to mother children I did not give birth to has given me a gift that I would have never known otherwise. It has opened my heart and strengthened my desire to mentor young women around the world. The experience even gave me the desire to design a positive t-shirt line and author a book on affirmations for women's self-empowerment, called "Girl with Game."

We never know where life will lead us, what unforeseen circumstances will cause our lives to change directions. My life direction shifted from my original plans, and that change allowed selfless love and kindness to take hold in my heart when these two girls came into my life. The experiences gave me a real opportunity to open my heart in adoration for all children, to support their development into adulthood, and to realize the need and the urgency to mentor children of all ages. All children are innocent beings who deserve unconditional love, nurturing, and support.

I hope that sharing my experiences will encourage men and women to become sensitive to, and more aware of, all the children who are put in their lives. We have the power to affect children in meaningful ways, and all children need love and compassion. They need praise, encouragement, and kind words. They need inspiration, guidance, and a nudge to move forward into their dreams.

It only takes a minute, a few kind words, or a simple deed to leave a lasting impression in someone's life. Who knows? You may say or do something prophetic that changes the life of one child, who goes on to change the lives of millions and millions of people. He or she could be the next president, a minister, or a CEO of the next technology company that changes history.

I hope both of my daughters do something special with the gifts they've been given, but I am extremely proud of the women they are becoming and I am thrilled to have the opportunity to love them as a mother. I am blessed to share the triumphs, challenges, and even the sad moments that have helped us grow as individuals and as a family. My journey has inspired me to care more, love more, and be a mentor to the younger generations.

Love is…

not the "I love you because you love me."

nor the "I love you because I want you to love me."

nor the "I love you because you are nice to me."

nor the "I love you because I want something from you or because you give me things."

No, Love is the "I love you just because."

"I love you for no reason."

Thoughts from Caroline

To love ourselves unconditionally, we must learn our own strength. Recognizing our own capabilities is the first step toward self-appreciation, which leads to self-approval, self-respect, and – finally – self-love. A sudden shock can propel us forward along the path of unconditional love in ways that no ordinary action could. When this happens, we are wise to appreciate the good it brings into our lives.

Affirmation

All of life's challenges are opportunities to grow in love.

Robin Craig

three-time Emmy award-winning television producer, author of the "Today's Widow" segment for the Hearst Corporation's Houston Chronicle, and host of "Robin Craig LIVE" on the Mingle Media Television Network

I became a widow in 2005, after a great 21-year marriage to my soul mate. My husband had undiagnosed cardiovascular and hypertensive disease, and he died suddenly and unexpectedly at the age of 43. At the time of his death, I already had lost my parents, my grandparents, all of my aunts and uncles (including their spouses,) and one of my five cousins, who was shot and killed at age six. Without anyone to ground me, my life instantly went into a tailspin.

To say I felt lost would be a gross understatement. I had been thrown into a chaotic abyss without an instruction manual to outline an escape route, and I truly had no idea which way to turn. I kept saying, "I just don't know what I'm going to do." I had always been confident and self-assured, but suddenly all I felt was scared and unsure. It was unsettling. One of my initial feelings was a profound insecurity – my bodyguard was gone. I was no longer protected. I felt so vulnerable, alone, and fearful. My future as I had envisioned it no longer made sense.

Then, in the second week of my widowhood, I experienced a premonition – something that had not occurred before and has not occurred since. My body jolted forward and I heard myself say, "I have to help the widows." The voice came out of nowhere, as if from someone else. I hadn't planned to say it, I didn't understand it, and, frankly, I felt a bit irritated. My life was in such an uproar - I was completely distraught and still in severe shock. I couldn't eat, I had no idea where I stood financially, and there was no one around to guide me. To think of others at such a time, when I could barely think of myself, was indecipherable. Nonetheless, every time something odd occurred or I faced a challenge, I'd think, "Well, there's another story to help a widow."

And, let me tell you, the challenges descended rapidly! I had water in my house twice, a home burglary, and an obscene phone caller. I weathered a Category 2 hurricane home alone, and I killed the world's largest rat … and that was just the beginning!

In 2010, I caught four opossums and four raccoons in my attic, something I never would have attempted while my husband was alive. In fact, prior to my husband's death, I ran as fast as I could to escape the presence of a mere grasshopper, cricket, or worm! Not only was I now capturing wildlife, my neighbor, Cindy, and I would subsequently take the critters down the street to the reservoir and release them into the wild.

Talk about female empowerment! I tapped into an amazing strength and determination I didn't know existed, and it was very reassuring. A sense of being able to do anything I set my mind to emerged with astonishing intensity, and I perceived it to be a beautiful gift.

In my career as a television producer, I went on to win three consecutive national daytime Emmys (2008, 2009, and 2010), the highest award in television. My many years of blood, sweat, and tears in the industry had culminated into national accolades by my peers, and I felt proud and grateful. A walk down the Red Carpet was no longer an event to be watched on television … it was a real life experience, and my only regret was that my husband was not physically by my side. He had unremittingly supported my career during our marriage and witnessed the hardships I had experienced, and his reaction to my three wins would have been likened to that of a proud new father whose wife had experienced a difficult pregnancy.

Although I can work anywhere in the country and make a great salary, I have altered my work habits and no longer feel compelled to chase television shows around America. Through intense loss and adversity, my life's mission has been born. I'm working for the widows! I feel at peace knowing I am fulfilling my life's mission, which is based upon unconditional love for others, especially those who are grieving.

There are 700,000 new widows annually in America, yet few know what to say or do. It's time for that to change. I never thought I would be the poster girl for widows (and widowers,) but here I am, and I feel so blessed to be doing this work. I've never heard anyone say it, but there's a 50/50 chance that every married person will become a widow or widower so planning for death is important.

In 2009, I founded "Help a Widow Day" and received a Proclamation from Houston's Mayor. I also began writing the "Today's Widow" segment for the Hearst Corporation's Houston Chronicle and hosting a weekly live web show, "Robin Craig LIVE," on the Mingle Media Television Network.

In 2010, I conducted a workshop called "Empowerment through Adversity" on behalf of a non-profit organization at Camp Widow, an annual event in San Diego, California. I feel very happy and blessed that I have been able to alter my career to help widows and others who have suffered a loss. I am told that I'm an inspiration, and that fuels me to continue working tirelessly to bring the topics of loss and grief to the forefront.

For example, a woman in Australia asked me to contact her dear friend in Chicago. She said her friend's husband had died four months before, and the new widow could do nothing except stay in bed and cry while wrapped in her husband's clothing in an effort to feel close to him. Another woman contacted me via my "Today's Widow" segment and said she had been compelled to read my work without understanding why because she was married. Then, without warning, the woman's husband committed suicide. I contacted both of the widows, and I remain in touch with them today.

It is a blessing that my work is available around the globe, and it's rewarding to know that I can provide comfort to those who are hurting. Life is different when you lose your spouse, but it can be good different. After experiencing loss, we have to seek new meaning and purpose in our lives. We have to find ways to reinvent ourselves and give back. Widowhood comes with excruciating loneliness. Like all widows, I face challenges regularly, but I'm a gal on a mission who is grateful for the opportunity to make the world a better place. My mission helps ease the pain.

I didn't have a desire or inclination to help others in this manner prior to my husband's death, and I believe a huge part of this work is due to the unconditional love that I now feel for the human race. I've come to understand more fully that every human is struggling with something – family, personal loss, health, finances, children, relationships. As a human, none of us is exempt from sadness and suffering. I had known that for a very long time, but it took losing my husband to make me fully grasp the essence of grief and the ability to feel love unconditionally for humankind.

I have learned that we heal through service to others. When we step outside of ourselves and focus on others, we find that our situation seems less severe. It's truly a life-changing catharsis. This work I'm doing has impacted my life greatly, and, as a result, I am more compassionate and more in tune with others. I can sense that, if I continue giving back and working for those who are in need, my needs will be met. I am at peace, and I feel in my heart that love is my driving force.

Not only am I working for widows, I am touched by others in need. I previously worked with a woman on a television show at Fox, and I knew little about her, but she was sweet and had a pleasant demeanor. I inadvertently found out through a social media site that she was a breast cancer survivor who had endured a mastectomy at age 26. At age 32, her two sons were 13 and 7, and the younger was struggling with his health. He had been diagnosed with a rare form of Lymphoma at age one, and the mother and son had taken chemotherapy treatments together, which is difficult to fathom.

I read that the boy's cancer, which had been in remission, had returned with a vengeance and that the family had lost their home due to medical bills. Since the boy was a minor, his parents were required to have a constant presence at the hospital and were unable to work. To add to it all, my former co-worker, who had been told she couldn't have any more children due to the chemo and radiation, found out she was pregnant and delivered a healthy, baby girl … a miracle baby! Sadly, however, the woman's husband couldn't handle the pressures and had moved away from the family. My heart went out to her - how much could one woman endure?

I chose to send love to the situation. I collected art supplies for the sick child, who enjoyed drawing, to promote his will to live. I found art stores to donate markers, paper, crayons, colored pencils, beads, leather, etc., and found other entities to donate clothes, diapers, and gift cards for the baby. Once the items were collected, I took a small group of friends, Kathleen, Cindy and John, to help me deliver the items, and we called ourselves, "The Blessing Brigade." It was unbelievably gratifying, and witnessing the family's reaction made all of the effort worthwhile. You could feel the love. I learned that when you give love, it is returned to you in greater proportions. There is no greater gift!

I'm no saint, and I'm not trying to prove anything to anyone. I just feel happy when I help those in need, and I feel immense love in my heart. I've grown tremendously during my years as a widow. I'm more forgiving, less judgmental, more appreciative, and eternally grateful for the lessons I've learned. I believe that unconditional love for others derived from adversity is what has led me down this beautiful path, and I count my immense blessings daily.

I never could have imagined I would learn to be grateful for the loss of my beloved family members, especially my husband, but I have. As painful as the losses have been, I have been gifted with a number of incredible, priceless gifts - the most important of which is unconditional love.

Thoughts from Caroline

To choose the path of unconditional love, we must include ourselves in the journey. Setting boundaries that limit behaviors and environments we feel are unhealthy is a step toward valuing the sanctity of our own souls. And, when we release our expectations that someone be a certain way or fill a certain role, we are blessed with the freedom to discover that we hold the very quality we thought we needed someone else to provide.

Affirmation

I offer compassion and set my own boundaries.

Unconditional love is about understanding that everyone is doing the best they can from their own state of consciousness. In my studies with Deepak Chopra, we talk about unconditional love a lot. It's so easy for us to get caught up with the idea that when someone else is doing something they are doing it to us or causing us some kind of pain intentionally. That is rarely the case. Usually people are acting out of who they are or what they know, and it doesn't really have anything to do with us personally.

We save ourselves a lot of pain when we can reach the understanding that all of us are doing our best. We don't take personally all of the things that are happening in the world. Once we understand everyone is on a unique path, once we realize that, we get to the point where neither flattery nor criticism changes who we are. Of course, we all like to hear good things about ourselves and sometimes get caught up in our desires to please people, but if we can stand from this place of knowing who we are, we can start to extend unconditional love to others.

Unconditional love starts with compassion. We haven't walked in someone else's shoes and had the combination of someone else's experiences and been programmed the way other people have. If we begin to understand each journey is individual and extend some compassion, it is easier to feel unconditional love for ourselves. It is a cycle - one helps the other.

We learn unconditional love in our primary relationships first. I came from a very large family - nine kids, all with different personalities - and we challenge each other in different ways. My main opportunity to learn unconditional love was in my relationship with my father.

My father is brilliant, a very talented attorney, a very successful entrepreneur, a person who is bigger than life, and a very loving,

loving man. But, he also has another side, a darker side; he has a very addictive personality. When these addictions come out, they affect all the people who love him and count on him.

When I came to the point where I felt like I had to parent my parent, the point where it becomes easy to feel resentful, I had to learn a tremendous amount of compassion as a human being. I had to come to the understanding that his role isn't just to be great for me. He is a human being. He is flawed; he is imperfect.

I am in his life for a reason as much as he is in my life for a reason. His addictive behaviors do mean he is not always going to be a leader in my life. I learned how to release preconceived ideas and righteous ideas about what love is supposed to be in our relationship. Being able to let go of these righteous positions and not having these certain positions keeps us from experiencing a lot of turmoil.

I have a vivid memory of a time when I was an older teenager. My father owned ski resorts and a restaurant and was the host of a couple of nightclubs. I was up at one of the resorts with a boyfriend, and I had my younger siblings with me. We were there to ski and help my dad with the businesses. I remember specifically that I was doing the best I could, trying to live a good life and to be a good daughter. One night, my dad was absolutely drunk out of his mind, and he asked me to give my siblings a ride home. It especially bothered me that my younger siblings had to see him like that. I felt like I was strong enough to see it, but they were not.

When we got in the car, my little brother started to vent and throw a tantrum. He said, "I hate him! I can't believe he drinks like that!" He came unglued. I had so much inner turmoil at that moment because I didn't want him to hate his father. Because he was in such pain, I found myself trying to defend my dad and tell him it was ok just to soften the situation, but, at the same time, I felt so much pain and resentment that I had to handle this situation. That my father would just exonerate himself from this responsibility and have me deal with these younger kids who relied on him for emotional and physical support epitomizes the challenge of addiction.

I talked to my father later, in what would become the first of many similar conversations. In the beginning, I thought, "I can help him. I can change him." But, sometimes you can't change someone. The important thing is to have boundaries. Unconditional love doesn't mean you have to accept all behaviors. You can love someone unconditionally and absolutely not accept behaviors that are unhealthy to you, that cause you pain and put you in difficult situations.

Do I deserve to be put in these situations when I do not choose them for myself? No, I don't deserve that, and I don't have to accept it. I learned to say, "I love you, and I want to be in your life, but if you are in those behaviors, I will not be anywhere near you." We have a responsibility to love ourselves unconditionally and say, "This is not ok."

We may want to spend time trying to reason with and control and be emotionally supportive to a person who is addictive – but they cannot just change their behaviors like that, no matter how much we want them to do so. There needs to be a catalyst for change; sometimes that catalyst is the recognition that their behaviors affect other lives.

My father and I have a good understanding now. I don't want to be there if there is going to be alcohol, and he honors that. I think it has modified his behavior a lot; he is more conscientious about it. Our relationship is very loving. When he is sober, my father is the most engaging, supportive, present person.

Honesty is one of the best gifts you can give someone who is struggling. I felt very liberated, very free, to have expressed my boundaries. When you express yourself, the other person sees your strength, and your strength gives them strength. The addictive personality does not have boundaries, it has difficulty with them, and when you demonstrate boundaries, it's like a light that shines into the person's life.

Your light will shine on everything and give strength to those around you. They will feel what your strength feels like. And, by setting those boundaries and loving yourself, you won't feel as threatened. You can still be loving and give them unconditional love without feeling threatened. You don't have to stop loving.

All of my dad's children have been much stronger in that area than he has been. I think he has learned so much from the strength of his kids. You really help someone just by holding that space and being the best version of you that you can be. You can really impact someone's experience when there is that unconditional love relationship.

The experiences with my father make me clearly discern what I do not want in my life and why. Because of my love for him, I can see the pain and the problems that it caused him very clearly. I feel thankful that I have that awareness. It is much easier to make the choice that I will not have that problem in my life. You can't change anything or make a great difference unless you are aware of what is really happening and why this situation isn't serving you. Having that awareness and being able to reach higher levels of discernment because of it has made my life much smoother, more peaceful, less problematic - and I am thankful for that.

It made a world of difference that my dad was never angry. My dad does love, is a very loving man, and he does so unconditionally. He tries to listen, and he loves his kids so much that even if I come to him with a problem, he is very receptive. For that, I am thankful. There are a lot of special things about him. I am sure I learned part of my ability to love unconditionally from him.

When he validated my feelings whenever I came to him, he gave me a level of strength that has served me in my life. I learned that no matter what happens, what I feel is valid, and it is okay to talk about it. And, it actually could effect some positive change. It gave me a lot of the strength I have to move forward in my family life and in my career. I give him a lot of credit.

Unconditional love starts with compassion. We expect the people we love to be perfect. When we remind ourselves - this is a flawed human being, just like I'm flawed - it reframes the whole situation. I think we can come out of it into a place of deeper compassion, and that is where unconditional love needs to start.

Thoughts from Caroline

One of the best gifts we can give ourselves is to listen to our inner guidance. Even though at times our earthly circumstances may seem to have a louder voice, our soul knows what is best overall and what is best for us. When we listen, the beauty of our life's path and purpose is laid out before us, and we are supported in ways we never would have thought possible. Honoring our heart's intent will always bring us to more unconditional love for ourselves and for others.

Affirmation

My passions open doors to love.

Tonya Fitzpatrick, Esq.

founder and co-host of award-winning "World Footprints" Radio and co-author of "Success Simplified" with Stephen Covey

Most people think they know what "unconditional love" is until they experience soul-taxing challenges that test their love. Three years ago, my husband and I discovered that our respective legal careers helped build our bank accounts but didn't nurture our spirits.

I loved politics and enjoyed keeping a finger on the pulse of national and international policies, but I had begun to find that the "political environment" could be distasteful. I was raised in the Mid-West and grew up with the belief that people were honest, friendly, and respectful. Throughout my legal career in Washington, D.C., I was blessed with the opportunity to meet some extraordinary and beautiful people, but I also witnessed negative transformations in others. I was shocked and disappointed in some of my associates' behaviors. I realized before my political appointment ended that I had a strong urge to reconnect with my belief in a common humanity. I was ready for a change.

While on travel to San Francisco, my husband and I met two sisters at a cocktail event and began to share our life stories. One of the sisters was a life coach, and, once she heard how dissatisfied and disillusioned we were with our legal careers, she posed some questions for us to consider: What things made us happy as a child? What makes us happy today? What do we love? What are we passionate about? We both knew we had a higher purpose and were intrigued by her questions. After we returned to our hotel room, Ian started to life coach me in an effort to discover my passions.

I told him there were two things that had generally brought me joy: horses and travel. As it turned out, travel was also one of his passions. We discussed the feasibility of starting a travel agency and agreed that there was great potential there. We were both really ready to do something we enjoyed and so we acted upon our idea quickly.

Within a month, we had filed articles of incorporation, decided on an agency name, developed a logo, and identified and partnered with a national travel agency!

There's a natural progression of events that occurs when one begins to faithfully pursue a passion. Things that are supposed to happen do happen, in the order and fashion they are meant to happen. From television appearances to the start of our award-winning radio show, "World Footprints," we experienced a lot of success in a very short period of time.

Dr. Rick Warren wrote a book about the "Purpose Driven Life" that became a New York Times bestseller. He tapped into and addressed a driving need that people have to make a difference and give something back. What we're doing with "World Footprints" is our purpose. We are encouraging socially conscious travel while fostering global citizenship and unconditional love. We're connecting the dots between culture, education, and travel, and we're spreading the news that we all share a common humanity.

For me, this work is important because I was blessed to grow up in a culturally diverse family. As a result, I never looked at skin color when I met someone new. However, I was subjected to racism, particularly as an adult. It hurt, but I realized that even the people who objected to me often overcame their perceptions once they took the time to talk with me.

For example, when I lived in California, I became engaged to a second-generation Italian man. His father, a first-generation Italian from Bari, loved me dearly. Unfortunately, my fiance's uncle Vito from New York seriously objected to our relationship. He asked, "What's a matter with you? Why you wanna marry this-a girl?..."

One year, between Christmas and New Year's Day, I flew out to New York to spend time with other members of my future family, and I finally met Uncle Vito. When I entered his home, I was greeted with a cool handshake. After a lovely meal together (a meal that Vito proudly cooked,) I was embraced warmly and kissed.

Vito and I became great friends, and, even after I broke off the engagement, I often would call Vito for a long talk. And, the man who would have been my father-in-law adopted me as his "God-daughter," and we maintained a close connection. Sadly, I lost both of these beautiful men a few years ago, when they died one month apart from each. I was blessed to have gained so much from these relationships, and I hope that they gained something from me.

From my experiences, I know that if we don't open ourselves up to new paths and new people, we miss opportunities for growth and development. There are so many beautiful people in the world! By learning about them, their cultures, and their heritages, we also can learn to accept and embrace each other's differences and finally eradicate racism. "World Footprints" is our first step toward this goal.

Within our immediate community of influence, we promote socially-conscious travel, global citizenship, and purposeful travel that leaves positive footprints by fostering cross-cultural understanding and friendship through the sharing of our common humanity. It is very fulfilling to promote authentic and transformational travel experiences that respect cultural heritage, the environment, voluntourism, peace through tourism initiatives, and travel philanthropy. Our message is one of unconditional love to our fellow global citizens, and we could not be happier in our pursuit to spread good will!

My husband and I love and support each other. Because of this we supported each other's decision to walk away from our respective legal appointments and chase our dreams. I don't believe that either one of us was fearful of failing because we believed in our hearts that we had a fantastic message and that we were doing what we were supposed to do. We both felt that "World Footprints" and the positive messages we share would fulfill our higher purpose.

Still, there were challenges.

Ian and I are very different people. He is laid-back and contemplative; I'm very energetic and intuitive. He is introspective and reserved; I'm quite gregarious and expressive. Since we had been producing and hosting our show for nearly two years before we jumped into full-time self employment, we had time to acclimate ourselves to each other's work styles and define each of our roles.

In the beginning, however, there were times when we didn't respect our respective roles as CEO and CFO. We tended to fight each other instead of fighting together. Eventually, we came to realize that our house would fall unless we built a stronger foundation. We began praying together, reading books together, and setting aside time to spend together on non-work-related projects. Most importantly, we began to fully appreciate the unique gift we've been given in sharing new travel experiences together through our work with "World Footprints."

Through the many challenges we've encountered, our relationship has grown stronger and richer. To make this work, we *had* to learn to give each other the space to be who we are. We both had to recognize and value the balance that we provide each other, instead of expecting to be married to our clones.

Acknowledging and accepting our differences also gave us the opportunity to more fully appreciate our vital similarities. We have the same values, goals, and interests, and we both genuinely love our family, others, and God. We know that God loves us unconditionally, and even though we succumb to anger and other negative emotions, we have always found our way back to each other because of this spiritual foundation.

Love that is without conditions makes room for forgiveness, and - in any relationship - the ability to forgive is imperative. The love in our home translates into a tremendous love for others, and this love is communicated through our messages. The fact that we are living a purposeful life with a meaningful message - to celebrate responsible travel, culture, and heritage and to engage the world as global citizens - has given us an amazing love for life, each other, our Lord, family members, and the global community.

Thoughts from Caroline

We've all been in situations where we felt different or "on the outside." Perhaps we looked or acted differently, thought differently, or hid a secret we felt no one would accept. We can choose to absorb pain from these moments, or we can choose to view them in a different way. Imagine for a moment that God wants to strengthen your belief in yourself: Could the universe create circumstances that would enable you to learn that belief? When we are pushed in a direction that is not comfortable for us, we learn to push back with an even greater force. These moments build who we are.

Affirmation

I appreciate differences and embrace similarities as a way to promote love.

Love Like God

Vida Ghaffari

actress, entertainment correspondent, comedian, and journalist

Today, I am a successful actress who is well known in the Middle Eastern community, both in the United States and abroad, but making my mark in the world was not easy. I had to overcome significant discrimination in Hollywood to find my own niche. I had to fight against typecasting and being forced into stereotypical roles. And, I had to make peace with my own childhood.

I grew up in a suburb of Washington, D.C. with kids who had names like Chad and Muffy and whose parents had country club memberships, kids whose parents bought them ponies for their birthdays. In addition to these disparities, I felt awkward as the only student in my kindergarten class and elementary school who was of Iranian descent. The other kids saw me as different, and this contributed to me having very low self-esteem.

I was always proud of my Persian culture and our rich heritage, but the attitudes of the kids at school made it extremely difficult for me to fit in with the other students. I was often left out of the group, and the other students would pick on me. At times, I even feared I would get beat up on the playground when no teachers were watching. I faced a great deal of discrimination.

When the political situation between Iran and the United States grew worse, the other kids became even harsher. It was as if the kids in my school related the violence in that country and the government's hatred of American ideals to me - someone who was born and raised in our great nation's capital and whose father worked for the U.S. government! Many days, I would come home crying. At those times, I would go to my calendar and anxiously count down the days until summer vacation.

The only time I can remember anyone standing up for me was one day when my mother brought a Persian treat, a powdered sweet bread, to my classroom. One of my classmates said, "Ew! Gross!" and I braced myself for derision and more comments like his. But, a half-Iranian student stopped them. He said, "They're not gross!" and then ate one. It changed the dynamic of the situation, and the rest of the kids began to eat them, too.

My parents taught me to ignore the treatment I received from the other kids, and, for the most part, it worked - until they would start again. I never resented the kids or blamed them, but I did feel sorry for their close-mindedness and wished their parents would teach them to respect others, as my parents taught me. While it always hurt, I understood their actions were a reflection of how they felt about themselves and that they were trying to impose those projections on to me.

As I grew older, I discovered many of those kids were from broken homes or had continual disciplinary problems, and it made me feel blessed to know that, especially through a difficult childhood, I had such wonderful parents. I feel grateful that I have smart, loving parents who instilled in me a sense of integrity. Without their boundless love, I never would have developed the high self-esteem and sense of self-worth that I have today. When I was able to look back on my childhood and send love to those who had hurt me, I felt so free and at peace with myself. Forgiveness is a wonderful thing!

Though I grew into an awkward teenager, the self-acceptance my parents taught enabled me to be happy I was different. I chose to embrace my strengths. Instead of focusing my attention on parties and being popular, I focused on my studies. Even in college, I was the quirky girl, but, by that time, I realized my uniqueness had its advantages: Everyone always remembered me!

I spent a great deal of time focused on journalism, and I even received a couple of writing and research grants on Capitol Hill, though I wasn't a journalism major. I pursued acting with the same zeal. I broke the mold of the cookie-cutter actress and felt empowered by my ability to pursue and create roles of substance.

Today, I am still breaking through boundaries and stereotypes, and I am happy that I am able to be a positive example of my heritage. I'm proud to have come so far and to have accomplished so much. I have appeared on well-known television shows and have starred in movies. I've even begun producing. It makes me excited that I can create opportunities for myself and other artists!

Over the years and through self-reflection, I have gained positivity and have come to love my distinct look in a town filled with tall, surgically-enhanced ingénues. Unconditionally accepting and loving myself, despite the harsh views of others, was essential in turning me from a girl with low self-esteem and little faith in herself into the confident and positive woman I am today. I am an example of the wonderful results we can experience by loving ourselves unconditionally, and, I can promise, it is amazing!

Thoughts from Caroline

Love is the strongest emotion. Even in the face of unspeakable tragedy, love is greater. When actions occur that seem to challenge our sense of what is good in the world, we have a choice where to put our focus. The knowledge that good can come from all, that good is in all, helps us make that choice. We can always find love and help it grow. We are called to love - it is our home.

Affirmation

Forgiveness is a direct path to unconditional love.

Lisa Gibson

global conflict mitigator, terrorism expert, attorney, mediator, public speaker,

and author

Four days before Christmas, a 20-year-old army specialist packed the last of his belongings into a medium-size suitcase and caught a taxi to the airport in Berlin, Germany. It was an exciting day for him, as he had been away serving his country for nearly two years. He was on his way home to spend Christmas with his family in Michigan. It was to be a long series of flights. First to Frankfurt, then to London Heathrow, on to New York City, and finally an arrival in Detroit, Michigan.

On December 21, 1988, the man's flight landed at London Heathrow airport to refuel. The earlier flight had been overbooked, and he was bumped to a later flight. The plane was only half full so he was looking forward to having some extra room to sleep on the overnight flight to the United States. He boarded the plane with the other passengers and settled into his seat. As he looked out the window at the ground crew going about their business, a suitcase was loaded onto the plane that was different from all the others.

The head pursuer made the announcement over the intercom with the final departure instructions: "Ladies and Gentlemen, I would like to thank you for flying with us today on this seven-hour flight to New York. The last of the luggage is being loaded onto the plane. In a few moments, we will be ready to pull away from the gate. Please take your seats, and be sure your seat belts are securely fastened and your seats are in the upright position. This is Pan Am Flight 103."

The plane pulled back from the gate, taxied down the runway, and revved its engines as it began to lift off from the ground and into the horizon. The young man looked at the ground one last time as it slowly became more and more distant and thought, "This will be the last takeoff before I once again plant my feet firmly on the ground in the United States."

At 19:00 hours local time, the last communications were heard from the plane. After that moment, my brother's life became a memory. In 1988, my brother Ken was killed in the terrorist bombing of Pan Am Flight 103 over Lockerbie, Scotland.

Prior to September 11, the 1988 Pam Am bombing was the single biggest attack on innocent American citizens. Long before the events that made "war on terror" household words, my family and I became actively engaged in the war on terrorism. Now, after almost 20 years, I know what it is to wage the battle in the physical and the spiritual realms.

After a lengthy investigation, a Libyan Intelligence agent was convicted. Libya accepted responsibility and paid civil damages to the families. As a Christian, I knew it was wrong to hate and that I was called to forgive. But, as I read the Bible, I was challenged because I learned it was about more than "not hating" my enemy, it was about *loving* them.

There are three verses that commanded me to love my enemies. Luke 6:27-28 says, "But I say to you who hear, Love your enemies, do good to those who hate you, bless those who curse you, pray for those who abuse you." It goes on in verse 32 to say, "If you love those who love you, what benefit is that to you?" Romans 12:21 further confirms this principle with the message to overcome evil with good.

So I made a choice. It was a choice few people understood and no one would have faulted me for if I had decided not to make it. It was a choice most exemplified by M. Scott Peck: "The whole course of human history may depend on a change of heart in one solitary and even humble individual - for it is in the solitary mind and soul of the individual that the battle between good and evil is waged and ultimately won or lost."

I decided that, rather than succumb to bitterness or simple indifference, I would respond in love. With the realization that love is an action, I began to look for opportunities to reach out in love to my enemies.

My first step was to send a letter of forgiveness to the man convicted of the bombing. The emotions were still fresh for me. *Would he receive the letter? And if he did, how would he respond?*

Even as I sat down to write it, I wasn't completely feeling the forgiveness in my heart. Frankly, it was simply an act of obedience. The Bible said that I was to "forgive" and "love my enemies," and I was attempting to do that in the most concrete way I knew how. So, I sat down with a pen and paper in hand and prepared to write. And I asked myself, *What do I say exactly? The guy is going to think I am crazy. Why even bother? Will he even be able to understand it?* All these were the doubts that ran through my head.

After wrestling with myself for what seemed like an hour, I felt free to begin to write. Since I couldn't speak or write Arabic, I had no choice but to write in English.

"Dear Mr. Megrahi . . ."

I introduced myself and told him my brother was killed on the Lockerbie plane - Pan Am Flight 103. "Only God really knows if you are responsible for this act," I said, "but, as a Christian, I need to forgive you."

It may have been one of the shortest and simplest letters I had ever written, but it was done. I sealed the envelope and addressed it to the prison location in Glasgow I had obtained from the Scottish Crown. As I drove to the post office, I had to wonder: *What effect would this really have?*

"I would like one airmail stamp to Scotland, please," I told the postal clerk.

I affixed the stamp on the envelope firmly, then held it one last time before I handed it over to the clerk to be mailed. As I walked away, I looked up to heaven and said with a sigh, "Okay God, I did what you asked. May your purposes be fulfilled."

Despite my doubts, the letter was delivered to him. Not only did he get the letter, but he actually responded to it in early July of 2004. I will never forget sitting in silence on the living room couch of my apartment. Just me, God, and the letter. *A letter from a terrorist in prison.* I tried to allow myself to appreciate the magnitude of that. *I wonder what it says? God, I hope it doesn't say something mean because I am not sure I could take that!*

I did not want to open it. I was afraid. But, I did open it. And I was surprised at what it said. It was a very kind letter, which expressed his condolences for my loss and shared verses from both the Koran and the Bible about how God answers prayer. He said he prayed I would be happy in my life and suffer no such sadness in the future.

Reading his letter validated my faith and renewed my desire to bring about change. I began to build a relationship with the new Libyan Ambassador to the U.S., and, in January 2005, I made a personal reconciliation trip to Libya. I met with individual citizens and government officials and, in each case, I simply told them my story: as a Christian I needed to come to get to know them so I could forgive them and learn to love them.

As I would share my story, time and again the walls would fall and even grown men would weep and say, "I will do anything I can to help you." I started to realize that my trip was more about them than it was about me. For the first time, I understood there is power in walking out what it is to love my enemies that breaks something in the spiritual realm. It breaks the power of pride.

As the walls fell, God's grace flowed. I found myself asking questions like, "What was it like when the U.S. bombed Tripoli in 1986? What was it like to live in Libya?" The responses I received were honest and heartfelt: "It is so good for you to ask. No one has ever asked me that before." After having heard about their lives, I came back inspired to do something to help improve their lives. Out of that experience, the Peace and Prosperity Alliance was birthed to provide humanitarian and education projects to serve the country of Libya.

On September 23, 2009, I expanded my understanding of unconditional love when I met with and forgave Libyan leader Muammar Gaddafi, one of the world's most renowned terrorists and the man many believe was responsible for the Lockerbie bombing. That meeting was a culmination of many years of striving to see the country of Libya change. It was a long, hard journey that came to a close for me as I sat face to face with the man responsible for my brother's death. I told him my desire was to focus on reconciliation with Libya by building a bridge of friendship between the people of the U.S. and Libya through goodwill and service.

It was a revolutionary approach when compared with the other victim's family members, many who had chosen to focus on bitterness and revenge. As such, the story of our meeting went around the world and was covered by nearly every large media outlet. Although there was criticism by some, the positive response far outweighed the negative.

My email inbox was flooded by responses from people all over the world who thanked me and asked if there were ways they could help with my work. I believe the response was so positive because when people see unconditional love in action, it is so compelling, they are drawn to it. On that day, the message that was communicated to the world was simply this: Daily there is a battle being waged between the forces of good and evil through love and hate, but, in the end, love always wins.

Thoughts from Caroline:

Regret serves no purpose. Action in the present moment does, and it is where we hold the power to put our focus. We are called to embrace each moment and bring it to a greater state of love, with the knowledge that we always do the best we can. Each moment, each challenge, each relationship is an opportunity to open our hearts. Hearts aren't stagnant – they either grow or they constrict. What will you choose for your heart today?

Affirmation

I love unconditionally NOW.

Jon Graves

*former professional baseball player with the Los Angeles Dodgers and
San Diego Padres and co-founder of SingleDad.com*

Jeseca was the dream wife ... gorgeous, sexy, and athletic; extremely talented; wise, yet humble; fun; energetic; supportive; and she loved the Lord with all of her heart. She was the heart and soul of our family, and it was her friendship, love, and support that helped shape me into the man I am today. Needless to say, the most difficult moment of my life came when I kissed her hand for the last time - the hand I held as she drew her last breath.

My heart skipped a beat the first time Jeseca smiled at me, the same, familiar beat it skipped each time she gazed back at me with her beautiful, blue eyes and wonderful smile. We met at a golf course bar and grill, fell in love shortly afterward, and were married nine months later. In our eleven years of marriage, we grew to trust and love each other more each day. And we dreamed of conquering the world in our own unique way - she would become the most recognizable portrait artist in America, while I played on the PGA Tour. Life was good.

That's not to say we didn't have challenges. Every marriage does. We just didn't allow them to overtake who we were together. We believed in *us*, and we believed in a mighty God who promised to make all things good, if we would simply put Him first. With that, we were able to rise above nearly every obstacle thrown at us.

Then, in the summer of 2003, nearly two years after a mini-vacation to see her family was cut short due to a tennis ball-sized lump under her jaw, our lives took a different direction than we'd planned, and our relationship and faith were put to the test.

When we were originally told she *might* have cancer, our initial thought was that God would use it to help us reach people for Him.

(Hey, we were young and ambitious and believed wholeheartedly in the dreams and desires God had given us together!) Our reaction to the actual diagnosis was a bit less enthusiastic, I admit. The transition from *might have* to *did have* was heavy. And, the outlook was dire.

She had what the doctors called the most advanced, localized case of cancer they'd ever seen. What began as a lump under her jaw became a massive disease -18 tumors - that affected every region of her neck. Our oncologist, a kind-hearted man who fell in love with Jeseca the moment he met her, found it hard to believe she was alive, and opted not to predict how long she might have left. But, he promised to give it his best shot and fixed on the goal that Jeseca would one day see her grandchildren play. And, then, as if to reprimand me for bad behavior, he turned and said, "Don't leave her. Most men leave when things get hard, and women lose hope. In this business, the people who die are the people who lose hope."

Men leave when things get hard. It blew me away. That wasn't an option for me. I loved her too much to leave her side, and our future together was on the line. So, with high hopes and an amazing God by our side, we began a four-year campaign to beat back an incredibly stubborn and rare form of cancer.

Simply put, it wasn't easy. They say the best chance at survival is an early diagnosis. When we found out that it was indeed cancer, she was already at Stage 4, the final stage of cancer prior to death. We were late in the game, and radical steps had to be taken to save her life.

Over the first seven months, she underwent an aggressive campaign of two simultaneous chemotherapies followed by seven weeks of daily radiation treatments, after which she had what was called a radical neck dissection. All went well, and it looked as if they had successfully rid her neck of the disease after the first year and a half. Unfortunately, there was another site that the doctors had become concerned about.

Halfway through that first year, we noticed that a miniscule lesion (tumor) had formed on her liver. The chemotherapies she was taking for the tumors in her neck had no effect on this particular tumor. As time went on, and as the doctors continued to scratch their heads, this three-millimeter tumor grew to envelop her entire liver and then spread to her chest, lungs, eye, jaw, lymph nodes, and finally back into her neck. It was baffling, but we never let go of the hope we had in God, or of the dreams we still believed would come true. **And, Jeseca never stopped smiling**. Jesus was her strength, and she sought His face even in the worst of times - in the early hours of the morning when she could give Him her heart without distraction.

On August 15, 2007, she was scheduled to have the second surgery in the span of a week to relieve the edema that had pooled around her stomach as a result of the tumor growth in her liver. I'd been working the midnight shift for a month or two so I could take care of her and the boys during the day, and, as I ran through the morning's dishes, I began what had become a routine prayer over the years. "Lord, please guide the doctor's hand in surgery and give him the wisdom he needs to treat her." For years, my prayer remained the same, and it was all about me: "Please tell the doctors what they need to know so they can give her back to me at the end of the day."

On this day, though, my prayer changed. We'd come a long way down this road together - Jeseca, God, and I - and God had proven Himself to us. So, as she carefully prepared to leave for the hospital, I knelt down and admitted that I was tired of praying out of concern. "Whatever happens today, I will always trust you."

Less than five hours later - as I clutched Jeseca's hand in the emergency room and urged her to come out of the coma into which she'd been thrust during the procedure - I watched helplessly in disbelief as her vital signs plummeted, and she drew her last, labored breath. Hours later, I understood, at least in the most fundamental way, that God had finished His work in Jeseca. Now, it was my turn, and my prayer had just become the impetus for the work God wanted to do in my heart.

Whatever happens today, I will always trust you.

My life changed instantly, and I had major decisions to make.
The most critical was whether or not I would bring the boys up to say
goodbye to the woman who was everything to them: their mother,
best friend, teacher, confidant, and protector of their hearts.

I look back on it now and realize the decision should have been easy.
In the midst of the emergency room atmosphere with physicians,
nurses, case workers, and hospice staff pooling around me, somehow
it wasn't. So I asked for five minutes alone with Jeseca, and, in that
five minutes, I understood the anguish with which Job must have
prayed as he ripped his clothes and cried out after he was told that his
family had just perished.

As I knelt down to pray and begin a new, lonely walk with God in
the middle of the emergency room, I knew the only opportunity for
the boys to heal was to allow them to say goodbye. I had no idea
what I would say or how I would hold it together when they got
there, but I trusted God would give me the right words at the moment
I needed them. He did. Under the shade of a small tree outside the
emergency room, I tearfully explained that their mom died there in
the hospital and was now with Jesus in Heaven. They were scared
and confused but brave enough to follow me, hand-in-hand, into
the emergency room, where they gave their mom their last hugs
goodbye.

Two hours later, after walking around the hospital campus chatting
and looking for lizards - something we'd done each day during her
second round of radiation treatments - we left for home without the
woman who made our family complete. After we walked in the front
door, exhausted and broken, we huddled together on the living room
floor. With the audio Bible playing and my arms wrapped around
them, the boys fell asleep within the hour. I cried until morning.

Whatever happens today, I will always trust you.

Life was a blur for the next two weeks. I had to handle the funeral
arrangements, burial, and memorial services, enroll the boys in
school, and think about going back to work. In the process, I had to

make the transition from husband and father to single dad, and I had to do it while the wound was raw and the sting was deep.

I've juggled two goals ever since: taking care of the boys and taking care of my heart. There's been many a night when I've stayed up until 4 or 5 a.m. to listen to the music we enjoyed together or to go through our journals and try to deal with the disparities between what we'd hoped for and the reality. It's been grueling, and I've given up some precious sleep, but my heart has come back to life with the help of a mighty, loving God. And, I've watched the boys begin to grow into extraordinary, humble young men.

The first few months were rough. Life was drastically different, and not only because we'd lost Jeseca. Now, the boys were attending school for the first time and were no longer able to spend every waking moment together. They had to deal with their pain separately. It tore me apart to think about it, but, as with everything else we had experienced over the past four years, God took care of it all when the time was right. Their hearts are healing now, too, and He's brought the three of us together in a way I never dreamed possible.

So what now? That's a question I've asked myself many, many times in the wee hours of the night. What was the point to all of this? What about that great work God was supposed to do in people's hearts? Perhaps He only needed to work on one.

Among other things, I've come to see that I had absolutely no idea how much Jeseca had to do and how much she was actually able to accomplish each day. Frankly, I don't think any man has a good enough grasp on how much women do until they're faced with the situation. It's laughable to think back on how far off I was when I would ask Jes why she didn't get to a small task during the day - seriously laughable. I get it now. **Guys, believe me - your wives are amazing!**

Do I have any regrets? Sure, but probably not what you'd think. We had a great marriage and a great friendship - better than most, or so I've been told. But, I've come to realize that while I loved Jeseca like crazy and poured all of me into her, I could have loved her *more*. I could have loved her in the small things of life. I could have read to her more while she lay on the couch with her legs up. I could have helped her more around the house, or at least I could have done it with a better attitude. I could have encouraged her every moment of every day to spend more time on her art than on my meals. Those are the things that make life richer, the things that make a marriage worth dying for.

I know I got some of them right, but I could have done better. **Every man can**. But, it's a choice we have to make every day **to serve and not to be served**. If we can do that, we will reap the greatest earthly reward God gave to man: the love and devotion of a woman's heart. Take my word for it - there's no greater treasure in all of the world.

Gayle Gregory

practitioner of fearless self-awareness and compassionate inclusion

---

All God

Consider for just a moment that it is all God.

That nothing besides God exists.

That the stranger we walk by is God.

That the person we despise is God.

That our enemy is God.

That the poor, the imprisoned, the ill,

and those different than us are God.

That the creek, the trees, and the birds are God.

That the smallest blade of grass, too, is God.

Can you love that much?

Thoughts from Caroline

Often we view love as a "search." We believe we have to go somewhere, do something, be a certain way to find love. What we discover on that external search is that love is inside of us and always has been inside of us. The journey takes us on a path toward our own hearts, where the greatest treasure imaginable resides. Every fiber of our being, down to the smallest particle of our being, is love. We have love. We are love. We provide love for the entire world, simply by existing.

I am love.

Diana Y. Harris

intuitive counselor and metaphysical teacher

Our forebears speak of a time before time was counted - when humanity knew we were a part of Nature and that Nature was a part of us. The face of the Divine could be seen in all of Life. Everything was family. This was our original wisdom. Some call this period the time of the Garden. No one can recall how long it lasted - only that the great illusion followed. It rolled into the Garden like a deep fog, which blanketed everything. The children of the Garden soon fell asleep from it. When they awoke, they could no longer see clearly, nor could they remember the original wisdom. For the first time, the children of the Garden felt lost. They became fearful and mistrustful. The belief in separation was born.

Not long after, the world outside the Garden began to glitter. The children of the Garden would sit transfixed by the spectacle for hours - no longer able to hear the Garden speak or to see her beauty. Her heart grew heavy as she grieved the loss of her beloved family. She knew her children must follow their own path. The days once spent in peace, love, and light were now dedicated to arguing the reasons why the world outside offered more than the Garden. The children were impervious to her sorrow and had become enraptured by the glitter. Tales of power and untold riches fueled their ambitions.

On the day of the children's departure, the excitement was so great that no one noticed the Garden moving quietly amongst them. She whispered her goodbyes and breathed a prayer into their hearts. Then she tenderly placed a spark of original wisdom there so they would one day remember. The children left the Garden unaware of the gifts that they carried within themselves. Their intention was to conquer the Outer World, because they now knew what it was to fear. Control was key, said a few. Wealth is power, said others. These would make things right and keep fear at bay, they thought.

For a time, the spark of original wisdom lived quietly in the space

*the Garden had created in each of her children's hearts. Throughout
the centuries, it passed from one generation to the next and to all
the children of man. The Garden stayed in communication with the
eventual millions of sparks in existence through the principle of
Oneness. She told the sparks to be patient for the time of humanity's
second journey and to rejoice in the little breakthroughs along the
way. These were signs that the race of man was growing into its
heart.*

*As the Garden shared her wisdom with the sparks, their radiance
increased, as did their capacity to give. The radiance traveled the
circle of sparks and returned to the Garden multiplied. We know
this to be the nature of Love, she reminded them. What we truly give
from our hearts returns to us multiplied. Love is not exclusive. It is
inclusive. The sparks flickered in agreement. The Garden cautioned
the sparks not to lose hope because their waiting had been long.
She reminded them that before all major shifts in consciousness,
humanity would first have to confront the brick walls that the beliefs
in separation created. This would be a challenging time for the
people of Earth, as it would initially cause fear and blame. These
impasses would have to be faced before the human race could move
into higher realms of awareness. It would take courage, forgiveness,
and compassion to heal the wounds caused by separation. And, it
would take the tenacity to rebuild.*

*The sparks now understood how they could facilitate the evolution
of humanity. There was much excitement all around. The sparks
began to flame brightly as their joy spread. "We were breathed into
the hearts of the people of Earth to help them actualize their Divine
Potential!" the sparks exclaimed. "And, we will help humanity to
remember Home. This will help them to heal the barriers to Love that
separation created!" they rejoiced.*

*The Garden was pleased. Her heart overflowed with gratitude for the
grace of the sparks and with compassion for her children on Earth.
She could feel that the time of remembrance was drawing closer. The
Garden closed her eyes and breathed a prayer into the hearts of her
children, for the second time. No one knows the date the sparks burst*

*into flame or the words of the prayer the Garden breathed into the
hearts of humanity – only that it did transpire that way.*

It is said among the elders that the people of Earth are now entering
the time of the second journey and that the light from the sparks of
original wisdom grows even stronger within us. They say the Garden
promised the people of Earth two signs that humanity was ready to
embark upon the second quest. It has been foretold that there will
spread across the sky a profusion of stars. Science may proclaim
them to be new planets. These stars will hold the light of our
forebears. They are the way-showers for our new journey.

The second sign will reveal itself much closer to home - within
humanity's own heart. It, too, will be subtle and then grow to affect
the masses. We will recognize the gifts of everyday heroes. They
will be catalysts of change. A new light will be found in the eyes of
the people. Strangers across the globe will come together in diverse
groups to collaborate in ways that serve the planet. These diverse
groups, united by common purpose and love, will help to redefine the
meaning of "family" and reignite within us the memory of our family
in the Garden.

All of these will be signs that humanity is beginning to awaken to the
heart of oneness.

The lessons of the first quest into the Outer World have been nearly
served. It has been a long trek laced with the many lessons of
separation. The people of Earth have begun to understand that faith
in money or false power structures does not ensure our survival,
growth, or happiness. This is an evolutionary step in healing. The
second quest of humanity represents a pilgrimage into our Inner
World and a return to our hearts. "This is a time when we must take
the most important Journey of all - that 14 inches from our head to
our Heart!" says Agnes of the International Council of 13 Indigenous
Grandmothers.

The ancients call this "the hero's journey." After much searching and
facing the dragons of fear, the hero returns to the place of beginning

(love.) The hero discovers that the answers and the treasures long sought in the Outer World were within him all the time, waiting to be discovered and shared.

It is love that urges us toward right relations with ourselves, our human family, with Mother Earth, and the Universe. It is love that gives us the courage to take the journey. And, it is love that leads our return home to our hearts.

Time for a Heart-ware Change

What does it mean to Love? I pause a moment to reflect upon what love means to me. I realize that my definition of it has evolved since the days of my youth. Thank goodness! I have discovered, along the way that love is not an emotion trapped in the chest. It is more than a feeling - it is an *awareness of ourselves and of others. It is inclusive rather than exclusive.* I think now that love is not fully love until it is allowed to express itself. Love is action, an outward affirmation of God within us. It has many faces - some are passionate, some may even be fierce, and others are soft in repose. Love comes in many forms but it only has one *heart.* And, we have never been separate from it.

It seems ironic that we live in the era coined the "Information Age," yet we accept so much disinformation as truth. It is time for a collective "Heart-ware" change. I think we have become confused, not by love itself, but by our vision of it.

On subtle and not so subtle levels, we have been led to believe that the love portrayed in childhood fairy tales, in romance novels, and in the sensation-driven dramas of television and tabloids is real. With these as references for love, it is no wonder many of us perceive ourselves as lacking, unlovable, alone, and/or not perfect enough. To add to this disconnect, the word "love" has been relegated to mean almost anything - a crush, a happy feeling, a rush of desire, and a myriad of other emotions. Love has even been used as a weapon, an obligatory and empty statement of affection, and as a standard closing on a letter.

We want to know what love is! Intuitively, all of us know there is something more to it. Our souls yearn for something deeper and more meaningful. We are a bit like Dorothy from the "Wizard of Oz," in search of the magic outside ourselves that never really left us. Dorothy, after quite a journey, made it home on her own with a bit of encouragement and faith. All of us are seekers searching for the love that feels like home. Like Dorothy, we will discover that love has been here, all along. It is the wisdom of our hearts, God, and our spiritual DNA.

We sometimes fail to recognize love, as it comes in unfamiliar packaging and sometimes on unfamiliar ground. This love asks us to *know ourselves* and to *fully participate* in the human experience – to embrace the gifts and the lessons of the light and the shadow.

I admit it is challenging to love the world in its current state of affairs, just as it is challenging to love *unconditionally*. Real love means to love ourselves and others un-split from our frailties, flaws, and gifts. It takes a great deal of courage, honesty, understanding, and forgiveness to be *present* for that level of loving. Are we ready to commit to love in a higher octave? I believe so. We are already on the path.

Dana Heidkamp

The Ride

Sometimes I see God like a carnival ride,

spinning around

as we clutch to His side.

Denying our unity,

only to succumb to

Him completely

for letting us ride along with Him.

Not because He lets us watch

or lets us play

but then judges a "wrong" way.

But, truly, for letting us fall,

bruising the knees He made,

and then helping us rise,

forgiving us before

we even screw up.

Thoughts from Caroline

We are surrounded by love. At all times, in every moment, love embraces us and envelops us. In our moments of need, we can call on love to support and comfort us. Understanding that love can arrive in infinite forms – from a loved one's guidance to a furry kitten at our doorstep – helps us to recognize its presence in our lives. When we open ourselves to love, it always finds a way.

Affirmation

Love is eternal and all-encompassing.

Unconditional love is a blessing when we receive it. A dog leaping up and licking our face when we come home, a hug from an old friend, a loved one bringing us soup and crackers when we're sick in bed - this is love. This is comfort. This is caring. And these are memories we carry with us - so important are these gentle touches of kindness. We remember the embraces and the wagging tails and the laughter long after the giver of these gifts has departed this Earth.

But does death break these bonds? Do the gifts end when the person or pet's mortal life has reached its end, and we are left behind with our grief and our memories? Or, do their spirits go to a place where they can continue to help us? Are there powerful "beings" of the saintly or Godly type who provide us with help and comfort from beyond?

I am a medium, and I can talk to the dead. Yes, I see dead people! I see them, hear them, and get pestered by them. The dead have plenty to say. They are constantly trying to communicate with us. And amazingly, they also try to help us out in times of crisis.

I can tell you from personal experience that we humble humans receive unconditional love and support from another place. The spirits shower us with help and guidance. They even send us warnings. Best of all, we are rewarded by the spirits for the good deeds and the kindnesses we have shown to others on this planet.

Remember "The Little Rascals?" That used to be one of my favorite television shows. I loved the antics of "Our Gang" and the shenanigans of the kids. Fast forward to adulthood. One glorious fall day, as I stood at my kitchen window and looked out at the crimson colors of the maple trees in my yard, I heard a frantic sound. It was a distinctive, plaintive "meow," the sound of an animal in trouble. I opened the door and went outside and tried to determine the source of the sound.

I wandered into my neighbor's yard and peered underneath her porch. There, huddled in a corner, was a tiny, grey kitten. It shook like a leaf and wailed like a banshee. Out of the corner of my eye, I saw a flash of orange and black zip by me. Another kitten! I rounded my neighbor's house and found three more furry little creatures hidden in the fallen leaves near her garage. I knocked on her front door.

"Hey, Marilyn, do you know you have four kittens hiding outside your house?" I asked her. Marilyn and I had always had a good neighborly relationship.

"I sure do," she said. "One of them kept me up all night with its crying."

"What are you going to do about it?" I asked her.

Her response surprised me. "I'm just hoping they go away. I don't want to feed them! You know what happens then! I'll never get rid of them!" I was a little shaken; she had always struck me as being compassionate. There was no mother cat to be found so the general consensus was that they were motherless.

The little, grey kitten continued to cry through the night. Cuddled up in the safety of my warm bed, I could hear it through the closed window. And, I decided that I couldn't let the situation continue. My beloved cat Spike had just died three weeks before. I had been having strange dreams at night after he died. As a medium, I frequently have psychic dreams, which are different than the regular, wonky, run-of-the-mill dreams we all experience. In one dream, Spike was alive and walking through the kitchen.

"Spike, you're dead!" I said in the dream. "What are you doing here?"

In English, he said to me, "I'm coming back. And - I'm bringing friends." As he said that, I could see a few feline fuzzballs go tearing through my house. But I had forgotten the dream as I laid there in my bed and listened to the sobs of the grey kitten.

The next day I went to the food store and loaded up with cat food. By jingo, I was going to feed those little guys, but how to do it without Marilyn seeing me? If she caught me feeding them on her property, our friendly relationship could quickly become icy. And the kittens were still under her porch.

Well, it gets dark early in late October. I waited for the sun to go down and darkness to envelop the neighborhood. I stashed several cans of cat food in my coat pockets and crawled on my hands and knees, through the bushes that separated her property from mine, until I reached her porch. From the light in her living room, I could see her as she watched "Jeopardy" on television. I peeled back the lids on the cans and pushed them as far as I could under her porch, then I slithered on my stomach back to my house.

And, that's when I realized I had left a trail of evidence. Back outside I went. I could hear the sounds of the kittens as they hungrily licked the remains out of the cans. I snatched the cans and crawled home. Mission accomplished! This went on for days, or perhaps I should say, nights. All I wanted was to get the kittens onto my property so I could catch them and take them to a humane shelter. No way was I going to take in FOUR kittens!

You know what they say: We make plans, God laughs.

Eventually the kittens figured out that the chuck wagon was at the house next door so they began to camp out on my property. They hungrily waited for me to open my back door every morning to feed them, but they kept their distance. I would see them as they frolicked in the piles of brown leaves I had raked and soaked up the last warm rays of October sun. It was clear these little creatures were full of mischief, and that's when I began to call them the Little Rascals.

One night, the temperature dropped to unseasonably low levels. The weatherman was calling for snow at a time of year when it usually just dropped into the forties at night. I could hear crying at my back door. I opened it, and, to my surprise, the Rascals scampered into my house, unafraid to be with me! The cold snap must have frightened them, and they knew a sucker when they saw one. "OK, just for one night," I said. "Tomorrow you go to the humane society."

That was seven years ago. Buckwheat, Alfalfa, Spanky, and Jackie never made it to the shelter.

Everything was fine in our happy home until one day, when a crisis occurred. The cats were now used to being house cats. Since I lived on a busy street, I didn't want to let them out. But, on this day, I opened the front door to get the mail, and Jackie, a big orange and white male, sprinted out the door and down the street. I chased after him, but he was gone. And he didn't come back.

Every day, I went out looking for him, but to no avail. I cried myself to sleep, but calling it sleep is too generous. My anguish at having lost Jackie made it impossible to drop off in slumber.

Then, one night, I had a dream. I frequently see dead people in my dreams, from my own relatives to friends to the loved ones for whom I do psychic readings. This time, I saw a man, but he was no ordinary man. He had dark hair and a beard and wore a long, brown robe with a simple belt made of rope. On his feet were crude sandals.

He emanated an extraordinary energy, something I had never experienced before. It was almost like an energetic, magnetic, or electrical force field that I could actually feel in my body as I slept. He *radiated* a calm power.

He said to me, "Jennifer, you have been kind to animals in your lifetime. Your kindness will be rewarded. We will help you find Jackie. You must go out looking for him, not in the day as you have been, but at night. He is near the house but will not come back to it. Be patient." And, I awoke, and sat bolt upright in bed, shocked. *Who WAS that guy?* I drifted back into a deep sleep, the kind I had not enjoyed in days.

When I woke up in the morning, a sense of discomfort began to

gnaw away at me. I had been raised as a Catholic but hated going
to catechism or Bible school. Those are my Saturday mornings you
are taking from me, Mom! What about my cartoons? Well, you can
force me to go, but you can't force me to listen! And, I did not. All
that stuff about the saints? Who cares! I had my doubts about the
parishioners who lit votive candles at St. Catherine's Church, who
prayed the rosary to their favorite saint.

My uneasiness deepened. "It couldn't have been ... no, it just
couldn't have been...a SAINT, could it? Holy - I wish I had been
paying attention in catechism!"

Had I seen animals at the man's feet, near his sandals? And wasn't
there a saint known for being the patron saint of the finned, furred,
and feathered? I called a friend, a practicing Catholic. "What's the
name of the saint who watched out for animals?" I asked her.

"St. Francis of Assisi. Why are you asking?"

"Never mind," I told her. "What does he look like? What does he
wear?"

Silence. Then: "Brown robes, with a rope around the waist and
sandals. He had dark hair and eyes."

I was now shaking in my shoes. Could it be possible that a saint
knew of my existence? Is there so much love for us on the Other
Side that the spirits there will help bring back a lost pet? I had never
helped animals in order to score brownie points with a higher power.
Was this for real?

I didn't have to question that again because the man continued to
show up in my dreams. Night after night, I drove the streets of my
town with my windows open, calling out Jackie's name. The man
in the brown robes had shown me railroad tracks in one dream and
what looked like a car lot. I had stocked the car with provisions: a cat
carrier, a blanket, food, water, and litter.

As I drove down a dark, deserted street one night, I happened to glance in my rear view mirror. And, then I saw it - an orange and white creature jumped out of a garbage dumpster. I quickly turned the car and tore down the road. I pulled into the driveway where the dumpster stood and where my skinny and bedraggled Jackie cowered in its shadow.

I noticed that I was in the lot of an auto body shop and that there were train tracks nearby. I slowly knelt down and called to Jackie. He seemed dazed, as if he recognized me but was frightened to come to me. Instead, he crawled underneath a chain link fence and hid underneath a car. It was no use. He wouldn't come to me.

At this point, I noticed the security cameras, which were positioned all around the car lot. I figured it would be a matter of time before the police showed up to ask me why I was pinned to the chain link fence. I needed a plan B. The next day, I went to the auto body shop and introduced myself to the owner. I told him my pet had run away, and I had found him there.

I also went to the neighboring homes and handed out my phone number. A woman named Barbara, who had cracked her door suspiciously when I knocked, saw the cat food cans bulging in my pockets and told me she would try to help. Her son had seen Jackie in their yard.

"Give me one of those cans," she said to me slowly. "We have an old animal trap up in the attic. It's a safe one; it won't hurt him. I'll put the food in there and see if we can catch him for you."

The next day at noon, my cell phone rang. It was Barbara. She had Jackie! After two long months of crying, driving, and searching, he was home!

Unconditional love? I know all about it. The kindness of a stranger, the surprise appearances of a saint in my dreams, and now the purring that I still hear, seven years later, as a rascally feline curls his tail around my leg.

Thoughts from Caroline

How can we understand the meaning of love, when we have bandied the word about like a ball? By remembering that love, in its essence, is absolute. We can choose to give the word the value it deserves and then act in a way that reflects its meaning. Extending this absolute love to ourselves and to others ensures a peaceful, happy life. We can radiate pure love because we are pure love.

Affirmation

" *The more I focus my thoughts on love, the more I will be able to act in love.* "

What is love? How can a single word encompass such a breadth of emotional states? Ranging from a mere generic expression of pleasure to the most intense and passionate declaration of emotional connection, each person grants this word its weight, context, and depth. I question my own intention when I claim to love a meal and then profess an undying love for my amazing children.

In pursuit of my own comprehension of love, I have struggled most with the range of purity embodied within this emotion. Do we belittle the notion of love by the arbitrary use of the word in casual context? Can we really say that we fully comprehend the intensity and sanctity behind this four-letter word? One could argue that this emotion is so dynamic and abstract that it is impossible to encapsulate.

Some people are quick to love and just as quick to let the love fade, thus granting the emotion less weight. Others tend to be frugal and guarded with their emotion in fear of getting hurt. Having experienced and experimented with both, there is an undeniable haze of apprehension and trepidation which clouds and restricts the true emotion. These perspectives on love share a common thread of conditional, self-serving interests.

Beyond mere semantics, the true emotion is absolute. Those who have loved purely and to their core know without question that it is as real and tangible as anything else in our perceived reality. As I have come to understand from my personal experiences, the purest form of love is completely altruistic, unconditional, and pervasive. As idealistic and unrealistic as that foundation may sound, this quality is immediately exemplified the moment eye contact is made with one's own newborn child.

There are other ways to understand the clarity of this emotion, but I had never experienced true love until the day I gave birth to my first son. When I was handed this tiny baby, I knew there would never be an obstacle, hurdle, or discord that could ever stop me from loving this being. The normal considerations one confronts when *mentally* grasping at the notion of love became completely irrelevant from that moment forward. It was then that I finally understood.

Love has nothing to do with reciprocation, gratification, or limitations. As I examined and assessed, I found that the greatest factor was acceptance - an open acceptance of oneself and others. As imperfect and dynamic beings, we present ample opportunities to disappoint those who impose limitations and conditions upon us in return for affection.

That being said, there are certain emotional states that masquerade as pure love, and most likely have an element within, but are hindered and tainted beyond recognition by contingent variables: love grounded by attachment or by lust. Both are selfish and sway on conditions, and both are a recipe for inescapable pain and suffering, which completely negates the purpose for loving. When love's foundation is precariously set upon the need to fill a void, a desire to be quenched, or an illusion to be validated, it cannot withstand the growth and depth necessary to reach skyward.

I began to reevaluate my existing relationships using this realization as a benchmark - my husband, parents, extended family, friends, pets, and every being I encountered along my path. I first embarked on this practice contemplating those closest to me, as those truths seemed more blatant and obvious.

Was my love for these beings hinged on expectations and requirements? If so, what attachments were causing me to project this conditional love? I found that the root of my restricted loving capability stemmed from a lack of self-acceptance. As I worked through this clutter of limitations, it became apparent that to ultimately accept others, one must first fully accept one's self - the infrastructure of pure love.

My driving force in this emotional endeavor was the conviction that, if I was going to love at all, I was going to love purely. There was benefit neither to the bestower nor the recipient to engage in this profound connection if it was only held together by the thin threads of conditions. I had savored this overwhelmingly intense quality of emotion with my children, thus, I knew it existed and could spread.

From these realizations and practices, an amazing occurrence then began to take shape - my love actually began to grow and expand. The fear associated with being hurt, being disappointed, of loss and vulnerability diminished. The foundation to this emotion shifted to a sublime and passionate appreciation for these beings in their own dynamic and unique states, completely independent of other factors, perceptions, or projections from me. I liken my experience of expansive, pure love to a constant 360-degree voluminous and unadulterated blaze, instead of selective, isolated, laser beams.

My practice continues to grow and spread. I now view my job, as the person radiating the love, to be compassionately understanding, to do everything in my power to end others' suffering, and to be an aid in their pursuit of happiness. There is absolutely no room for fear or pain in this equation, for without imposed requirements, expectations, judgment, and need for reciprocation, one is free to love in the purest form. This is how I have come to love my children, family, friends, and this is my ongoing practice for every other being I encounter.

May we all pervasively radiate in altruistic love, free from the constraints of conditions and limitations, and open to all beings on the basis of absolute acceptance, genuine compassion, and the pursuit of complete understanding.

Thoughts from Caroline

Through the empowerment of ourselves, we are able to empower others. And, through unconditionally loving ourselves, we can unconditionally love others. Trusting that all is right – every situation, every person – frees us from the emotions that can pull us toward negative thoughts and actions. This trust enables us to live in a state of unconditional love.

Affirmation

I choose positive thoughts and emotions.

Dr. Matthew B. James

President of Kona University and its training and seminar division, The Empowerment Partnership, where he serves as a master trainer of Neuro Linguistic Programming

A few years ago, my wife came to me and said as sweetly and kindly as she could, "Can I tell you something? You're a little overweight." As someone who spends all my time teaching people to be healthy in all areas of their lives, I knew she was right. She was demonstrating her unconditional love for me by telling me the truth in a loving way.

At the time, I was 235 pounds (at least that is what I told myself - I think it was more.) That would have been fine if I were 6'2". But I am 5'8", and, according to medical charts, I was obese!

My grandfather told me when I started teaching, "When you talk, it's *your* ears that are the closest to your mouth so the first person who should be listening to what you say is *you*." I needed to apply the tools that I teach to my own situation and take action to lose weight. That led me to a deeper realization.

I already had unconditional love in my relationship with my wife. Waking up to the fact that I was not in perfect health made me understand that I needed to learn to love myself unconditionally. Only then could I truly "walk my talk" and make the changes I wanted.

As president of Kona University and The Empowerment Partnership, the university's training and seminar division, I teach Huna, the ancient Hawaiian system of energy and healing. One of the fundamental principles of Huna is that we become "pono" with ourselves. Pono is a Hawaiian word that means to make things right - not as in "I'm right, you're wrong," but right with each other and the situation. Pono is a feeling of congruency and calmness to the extent that nothing needs to be said. When applied to your feelings about yourself, to become pono is to love yourself unconditionally.

If you constantly criticize yourself, you undermine your efforts to improve yourself. Only when you overcome negative emotions and limiting beliefs about yourself can you truly become pono in a way that empowers you to achieve your goals and be pono with others.

The Huna process of forgiveness is called ho'oponopono, which literally means to make something doubly pono. In doing research for my dissertation, I found that those who engaged in ho'oponopono experienced a statistically significant reduction in unforgiveness compared to a control group. This research was the first time ho'oponopono has been studied as a process-based approach to forgiveness. It validated this method as an effective therapeutic approach for improving relationships and mental health.

There are many different approaches to ho'oponopono. My book, "The Foundation of Huna: Ancient Wisdom for Modern Times," focuses on a process used for hundreds of years within the lineage that I carry. This form of ho'oponopono takes place on the mental plane - you mentally disconnect from the old way of being with a person and then create a new relationship. This is an ancient variant on the modern process known as Neuro Linquistic Programming. NLP is a set of guiding principles, attitudes, and techniques that allows a person to change, adopt, or eliminate behaviors and choose mental, emotional, and physical states of wellbeing.

Sometimes it seems easier to change our feelings about other people than it is to let go of long-held negative feelings about ourselves. One way to do both is to realize that negative emotions toward ourselves and others are two sides of the same coin.

When you look in the mirror, what do you say to yourself? Most of us talk worse to ourselves than we ever do to others! You cannot do that and be pono. Yet being pono is key to breaking the hold that negative self-talk and limiting decisions have on our ability to grow and change. In the same way, as we release negative emotions about ourselves, it frees us to truly love others.

If this sounds like just a bunch of self-affirmation, think of this: When you are on an airplane and the flight attendant gives the safety talk, they always say, "If an emergency occurs, make sure you put a mask on yourself before you put it on someone else." There is a reason for that.

It's the same with parents and other caregivers. I have two kids, and I know that in order to take care of my kids, I have to take care of myself. In fact, each reinforces the other. The better I care for myself, the better I am able to care for others. And the more I love myself and others, the easier it is for me to be gracious, forgiving, and truly pono.

At its essence, Ho'oponopono is grounded in the idea of unconditional love. Forgiveness is not just a byproduct of learning to love unconditionally - it is a requirement for learning to truly love others and ourselves.

Thoughts from Caroline

We can erase the words "mistake" and "failure" from our vocabulary. We can choose instead to view every action as an experience for growth. Consequences are corrections, and our next actions can always be influenced by what we have learned. We can choose to grow as quickly as our soul desires by recognizing the lessons that present themselves. We also can choose to release others from our projections and recognize that they, too, are on a path of learning.

Let go of judgment, criticism of ourselves + others

Affirmation

Loving myself is the beginning of all the love
I can offer.

Love Like God

Jacquie Jordan

author of "Heartfelt Marketing: Allowing the Universe to be Your Business Partner" and owner/founder of TVGuestpert.com

Unconditional Love! In its simplicity, it's all we are. It is the simplest, purest form of being ... our true essence. However, in our human condition, unconditional love is a practice that is not always easy to allow because it is an allowance of all that IS.

We are living in a time where relationship models and the concept of romantic love are shifting. We are re-writing our belief system to understand that love is not simply a feeling. It is a decision based on commitment. We may not always feel love or feel loving, but we can choose to act in a loving way. We can also choose to harbor loving thoughts about ourselves and about others.

This new paradigm is revealing that we live love. We live love in our thoughts and in our actions. And, most importantly, we live love in our hearts. If those are aligned in right being, then we feel the emotional benefit – bliss!

By the time I was thirty-one years old, I had two "failed" marriages. Though some might have given up the search for love, I was a romantic. I refused to give up on my dream of love, of finding my soul mate. Instead, I chose to embrace my "failures" as growth lessons. I wanted to learn from my mistakes in the hope that my next relationship would prove lasting. But, even though I was determined, I struggled with how I could promise my life to someone when I could never know what the future would bring. I searched for the answer to an age-old question: How can love last?

I found my search was not an external one, not outside of myself. Through extensive work within, through an internal unwinding of emotions and ingrained thought patterns, I discovered the answer had been residing in my heart all along. In that moment I understood: It wasn't about the person I loved or our situation. Love does not define itself by external circumstances. It was about *how* I loved. Through this self-reflection, I came to an understanding of the kind of love I wanted to *give*.

I desired to love unconditionally. I wanted to allow myself, my partner, and our relationship to exist "as is," without expectations and conditions hiding around every corner. I wanted to love, not as a way to get something or have my needs and desires fulfilled by one person, but as an expression of commitment. Recognizing this desire led to my understanding of what unconditional commitment can look like.

As I practice this act of unconditional love, through a new gift of a relationship with my beloved, I continue to grow. I have learned that the best I can be involves continually showing up in a practice of unconditional love and acceptance.

I have chosen to make these promises of love:

I will be the best girlfriend/lover to my beloved that I can be, not in comparison to his past girlfriends, but in comparison to my past selves;

I will strive to be fully present and available;

I will allow my beloved the room to exist as himself without any judgment or motivation of my own expectations;

I will take care of my self – physically, emotionally, financially, and spiritually – so that I am able to participate in our relationship as a whole and complete person;

I will support his ideas, his path, his dharma, and his growth, to the best of my ability;

I will remember to have fun with him – to laugh at the little, simple things that deepen our connection;

I will choose to be consistent in time, space, and communication that trust continues to grow;

I will recognize that he is a man and I am a woman and that we are different – and honor those differences;

I will speak up when I am not in the place within myself to meet any of the above practices;

I will be patient when we are both standing in un-centered spaces;

I will let him know every day how much I love and adore him, and – more importantly – how much I LOVE loving and adoring him.

As a culture, we've used love as a hostage, and I was no exception. We have taken our loved ones and our family members and held them hostage to our concepts of who we think they should be. We have told them our ideas of how we think they should live, and we have made clear how they should treat and respond to us based on our preconceived concepts of ourselves. If all of these conditions were met – if they complied with our wishes – then we "loved" them.

The beauty of pure, unconditional love is that it does not hold any of these conditions. It opens our hearts and our minds and expands our concept of how we have loved. Loving for the sake of loving is our beginning, the shift in consciousness that will allow us to move toward unconditional love. And, as we are human, we must extend this same unconditional love to ourselves with the understanding that we may not always reach this unconditional love ideal in every moment.

Unconditional love is allowing others to be who they are without judgment. Unconditional love is holding space for others to be who they are and holding space for yourself so that you can unfold into the cosmic deliciousness of your own being and life. Unconditional love is a release. It releases all expectations, all selfishness, and simply accepts. Yes, it is simple. Yes, it is everything!

Thoughts from Caroline

We can choose to reinforce others' perception of unconditional love by being an example of it. We can also choose to verbalize our unconditional love and support. Encouraging and inspiring another to believe in the possibility of unconditional love reinforces our own belief. Through these types of unconditional relationships, we are provided a safe foundation from which to grow.

Affirmation

I choose to offer unconditional emotional support to myself and others.

The relationship that has taught me the most about unconditional love is with my mother. When I was small, my mother gave me approval and appreciation consistently for everything I did. For example, she would acknowledge a seemingly small thing, saying, "I am so glad you put your Barbie dolls away in such a neat way." Or, when I was sitting at my desk doing homework, she would kiss me on the head, pat my arm and say, "I am so proud of you."

As I grew older, she would offer statements like, "I am so proud of my daughter. You are so brilliant and so capable and becoming so independent." Now, she watches every television appearance I do and says, "You expressed yourself so beautifully," even when I critique myself. She would always verbalize things in very positive ways – which I know as a psychologist is the perfect way to encourage a child and build self-esteem. Her words ring in my head with reassurance if I regret or worry about what I said or did: "If you said that or did that, it was the right thing to do or say in that moment."

When I was seven years old and going to camp for the first time, I was late to arrive, and, as a result, got the last bunk. It was dirty and filled with bugs, which made me cry and insist that my father take me home. Once we left, I felt badly. But my mom reassured me and said, "Of course, you're upset! You don't have to go back today, but how about going back tomorrow and seeing if you can get a different bunk?"

Looking back at this with my now-psychological eye, I see that the positive growth experience was that instead of dismissing my concern, my mother acknowledged it was reasonable for me to be upset, and, in addition, she modeled a way to solve problems. Her reaction paid off: I felt confident enough to go back to camp the next day, they gave me a new bunk, and I had the greatest summer!

From a psychological perspective, when parents love conditionally, the child is expected to behave a certain way to please them. The child perceives an underlying threat: if I don't act the way my mother wants, I won't be loved. The result is that the child becomes fearful and unable to trust relationships even into adulthood.

I am particularly grateful to my mom for being able to love unconditionally, since she did not have such a model for herself while growing up. In her generation, rules about how people were supposed to behave were much more a part of life.

Unconditional love from my mother means that she loves me for who I am and not who she wants me to be. She may say, "I would like you to do this, or to make this decision, or to live this way, but I also know you are your own person and that what would make me the happiest is for you to be able to decide for yourself." Or she might say, "This is not the way I would do it, or what I would hope for you, but I appreciate that you are making an independent choice. And I feel good that I brought you up that way." By her talking this way to me, I know that I am loved for who I am, and while all my behaviors may not be acceptable or desirable to her, I know that I am loved as a being independent of my mother.

This is in contrast to what many other children experience from parents, who commonly have their own ideas about how they want their children to live, whom to marry, and what career to choose. But, when those ideas are imposed on children, the youngsters do not grow up with a solid sense of self or of confidence. Instead, they can feel suffocated, resentful, and fearful of intimacy. Psychological literature notes unconditional love as a healthier form of parent-child interaction, whereby the parent loves and champions their children for who they are as individuals, allows them to develop their independence through their own choices, and appreciates their ability to define their own person.

While I feel grateful to have experienced an example of unconditional love, I don't always feel I extend that to others. For example, I do have expectations of others that, if not met, can leave me disappointed or frustrated. But, I welcome the challenge to be consistently non-judgmental and accepting, especially given that I live a complicated life in stressful New York and often travel internationally, where I encounter many different cultures. Since I work with many children, I am extremely aware of how I talk to them; I can disapprove of what a child may do but not of him or her as a person.

Adult relationships deserve unconditional love, too. When people make mistakes, they can feel guilty and sensitive, which requires that we be sensitive to what we say and avoid making the other person feel humiliated or unloved. This was keenly evident to me on the occasion when my friend's husband was driving me to my husband's funeral and took a wrong turn. Stressed about being late to such an occasion, I blurted out, "I told you to go the other way!" which made him defensive and angry. I quickly had to correct myself and say, "I greatly appreciate your driving and know you, too, are under stress. I may be worried about being late, but we'll get there."

Another relationship that taught me about unconditional love was with my husband. Our unconditional love was founded in the feeling of being soul mates so we knew we loved each other at the core of our being. Yet, at times, our individual styles led to feeling criticized or judged, since we differed in our styles: as a lawyer, he approached situations in a factual way, and, as a psychologist, I am far more emotional.

The challenge to unconditional love was evident on an occasion when on vacation in Hawaii. When he jumped over a cliff into the ocean, I couldn't spot him and became hysterical. When he reappeared on land, he looked at me sobbing and asked, "Why were you so hysterical? I was fine." This made me feel misunderstood and unloved. My challenge was to remember that differences in style about how to approach situations do not undermine unconditional love.

In this quest for unconditional love, I am aware I must also extend it to myself! Having high expectations for my own behavior, I can be hard on myself and distraught when I think I made a mistake. On those occasions, I have to catch myself and tell myself that I am still a worthwhile, caring person.

Feeling unconditional love, and extending it to another, can come naturally, but it also can be learned. In my work as a psychologist with clients, I help them learn to separate their reaction to a person's behavior from how they feel about a person by eliminating judgment, being understanding, and feeling empathy. Techniques to achieve this include compassionate communication and dialoguing. By listening to each other's narrative without criticism and negativity, we appreciate the other's point of view and are much more able to find common ground.

I apply these same principles and processes in interpersonal relationships to the international and intercultural work that I do, since I have learned that unconditional love and acceptance starts at the microcosm and expands out like a circle to the macrocosm.

As such, I am so grateful to my mom.

Thoughts from Caroline

What does it take to love? Is it an action we take, or a word we speak, or a thought we think? It can be all of these or any of these. But, love also transcends the usual human experience and envelops the soul. Our soul unconditionally loves. In each and every moment, even when our human form falters, our soul loves. When we are presented an opportunity to experience unconditional love at a soul level, we are truly blessed.

Affirmation

Love transcends my body, as it is the state of my soul.

I thought I knew what unconditional love was until I had a child, a daughter named Danielle, who almost died at ten months of age from spinal meningitis. We were lucky. She is now 22 and living life as a beautiful young woman with no side effects from the disease.

As the years have passed, I discovered there are various levels of unconditional love, much of which I have learned through my mother and her journey with memory loss. Mom is now in her end stages of Alzheimer's disease. I know it may sound strange, but her illness has been a gift to me. I have learned there is nothing more valuable in this world than to give or receive unconditional love.

Below is a story of one moment, one gift of unconditional love I call, "The Payoff of Faith:"

It had been weeks since the sun had been out. There was a softness, a joy, a simplicity that embraced everyone on this gorgeous, sun-filled day. You could see it in people's smiles and in their sparkling eyes. You could hear it in their chatter, feel it in the breeze, and in the calmness of your own heart. Oh, yes, there was an undeniable change in the air, and the sun was the spark! Nature's beauty was coming on strong, and this was going to be a blessed day. Even my mother, in her end stages of Alzheimer's disease, appeared to sense it.

As I walked into her room at the nursing home, I could see her shadow through the drawn curtain. She appeared to be taking a nap, and the light sound of her snore confirmed it. As I rounded the divider, I saw the curtains were drawn back on the large picture window, and Mom was basking in the sun. Her eyes were closed. She looked peaceful and calm, her breathing shallow but steady. There was a smile on her face, and the sunlight seemed to warm her soul.

Good, I thought to myself. *No fear, No worry, No pain*. I spoke to God and thanked him for the peaceful state Mom was in. I, too, smiled, and breathed a sigh of relief.

As I looked down from my mother's sweet smile, I saw her blouse was hiked up just below her breasts and her elastic pants, now way too big for her, were just below her belly button. Mom's full round tummy was exposed to the warmth of the sun.

"Hey Mom," I said, "Do I need to pull out that bikini for you?"

My mom's eyes twitched as she slowly opened them. She giggled like a small child and said, "Oh, no, Lori, I don't think I should be wearing a bikini." Then, she giggled some more, closed her eyes, and fell back to sleep.

She knew who I was! I smiled to myself at her playfulness and was amazed she said my name. I had not heard her call me by name in ages. I didn't even remember when the last time was, perhaps two or three years previously. Over the years, I had told myself my name wasn't important. It was about Mom feeling comfortable, safe, and happy with me - but today it mattered. My eyes flooded with tears, and my heart raced. What a gift my visit at that moment was!

I sat on Mom's bed, and crocodile tears poured down my face. My right hand gently rubbed her belly, back and forth, back and forth. *Wow,* I thought. I knew Mom had been losing weight. She could no longer feed herself, and all food was peer aided. I knew she was only eating 25 to 50 percent of her meals. I could see the weight falling off her, and the staff would inform me of her weight loss. But, that day, things were different. As I sat on her bed and rubbed her naked belly, I saw what appeared to be a hernia. It looked to be half the size of a melon. *How could I not have noticed this?* I thought to myself. *I suppose because she was always dressed when I saw her,* my mind responded.

Prior to this moment, it was just weight loss. But, it was now so much more. The 80-pound loss, the hernia, and the bagginess of her clothes said, "Mom isn't going to be around much longer." The disease was nibbling not only at her mind and her soul but her physical body. Alzheimer's disease was winning the battle. I had known it all along, but that day it felt so permanent, so imminent.

My mother had been in a nursing home since 2001. She wasn't formally diagnosed with Alzheimer's disease until the mid-90s, but the memory problems started years prior. You would think I would have had a grip on all this by that time, but, no, I just sat on her bed and bawled. My heart felt like it had been drop-kicked one more time.

How many times have I said goodbye to yet another piece, another phase of my mother's life? Of my life? How many times have I said goodbye to a part of this wonderful woman I love with all my heart? How many more times are left? The questions wouldn't stop, and my mind kept spinning.

I had an overwhelming sense of loss. Bit by bit, the phases of this disease held excruciating pain for me. I continued to weep and rub her belly as I prayed for guidance, for peace, for reckoning within my own soul. No amount of time is enough time to deal with the loss of a loved one, not even when you had years to prepare.

Then, with no warning, God spoke to me clearly, "Lori, you had one more connection, one more great story, one more wonderful memory of your mother. For that, be grateful. Today it was the bikini story. Tomorrow is an opportunity for another story. Just embrace your mother. Do not judge. Do not try to control the disease or the outcomes, just capture the moments, Lori. Write them down. Share what you have learned. Find the gifts wrapped inside the pain. Learn the lessons of the pain, Lori. Learn the lessons."

My body trembled at God's words, and tears poured down my face like a faucet. My shirt was soaked. My eyes were so puffy I could barely see, but my heart was once again filled with hope from His guidance.

As I left that day, I realized two things:

One, Alzheimer's disease destroys individuals as we know them, multiple times on multiple levels. You can look at this disease as painful and as one loss upon another, or you can look at it like a cat with nine lives, each being different but each offering love and comfort. The lesson is to learn to love unconditionally throughout the many stages of life.

Second, a friend of mine once told me she was jealous of the great relationship I had with my mother. I looked at her, baffled, and asked what she meant. She said, "My mother is healthy. She lives out of state. She is doing well, and, for that I am grateful, but I don't have the beautiful stories and memories you have with your mother."

Then, she paused a moment and continued, "Funny isn't it? I'm just not as connected to my mother as you are. Illness did that for you. Alzheimer's disease created that gift for you." We then smiled at one another with an inner knowing and respect.

Each day since the bikini incident, I try to embrace every moment with Mom. To love her. To thank God for all the gifts in my life, even those wrapped in great pain and discomfort. I know each is a memory. Each is a piece of her. Each is a piece of me, and these memories cannot be taken from us. How I choose to look at these moments, how I choose to live my life will determine the memories I create not only for myself but for others in my life.

Every day I look for the opportunities within the obstacles before me. I try to stay calm, peaceful, and still, yet alert, looking for clues to remove the pain, the fear, and the discomfort for both of us. My goal is to strengthen my ability to do this so we can both live life to the fullest.

Some days I admit, the chaos wins out. I crumble and cry. I lay broken as the cookie crumbles a bit more, and then another moment passes. Another day arrives, and I feel the warmth of the sun and I am thankful for the nine lives that live within each of us. I am thankful for the many levels and stages of unconditional love.

I savor forgiveness from others and myself when I become selfish and get side-tracked with my own needs and emotions. I have learned to love myself unconditionally with all my faults, knowing I can improve in future moments.

Here are the levels of unconditional love I have identified:

1.) **Loving someone else so much we forget life before them.**

This could be a child, a spouse, partner, or friend. Although we may not be able to imagine our lives without this person, most of us will have moments of disappointment, frustration, and downright anger when things don't go our way. We routinely lose our grip, and unconditional love gives way, as we are still living life by a plan of how we think things should unfold.

2.) **Loving someone who is temporarily in need.** We will do everything in our power to help them, comfort them, support them, and reduce their fear and pain. This could be someone we love who becomes ill, or who needs our assistance to complete a task, or who has gotten into trouble … During this time, we may have lapses in our love being unconditional. This might be due to lack of control over the situation or when the outcome we are working toward does not meet our needs.

3.) **Loving someone who is ill or dying.** We are willing to accept their condition or fate for what it is. We encourage them to live their best possible life and continue to be a part of their life throughout their journey. Here again, we may have lapses in our unconditional love when we focus on our feelings and our needs versus theirs.

4.) **Loving someone, consistently focusing on three things: Are they safe? Are they happy? Are they pain-free?** By doing this, we focus totally on their joy. Our focus is on them and them alone. We no longer judge their decisions, their reactions, or their outcomes. We just love and support them on their path, realizing it truly is their journey and not one we carry the burden of changing.

5.) **Unconditional love for one's self** is sometimes the hardest to achieve. Turning off the inner critic that bruises and attacks our ego is difficult at best. Instead of turning off the inner voice, sometimes it's easier to let go of our ego. By doing this, the hurtful words and thoughts pass over us. Our soul protects us with its confidence in us, knowing we are in control of our future, which allows us again another opportunity to love unconditionally.

I believe there are few people able to love all those they encounter unconditionally, but it is a wonderful goal and an amazing gift, even if it happens one moment at a time.

Thoughts from Caroline

Especially as children, we can become conditioned by our environments. Thankfully, we can consciously choose to re-condition ourselves. We are able to do this without harboring resentment or guilt because we appreciate that every so-called negative action directed toward us and from us allows us to experience a new aspect of growth. We can realize that each step we take toward unconditionally loving ourselves builds upon the one before, until one day we realize we have pieced back the fragments of our heart.

Affirmation

I value and love myself.

Sharmen Lane

author of four books, including "Giving You the WOW and the How,"

and life-changing inspirational speaker who has improved the lives of thousands

throughout the world

Unconditional love … for the majority of my life, that concept was completely foreign to me. For years, those words had no meaning to me, and I found the idea to be almost inconceivable. Like many, I grew up in an environment that seemed to be the epitome of dysfunction. And, in that dysfunction, I felt that love, if given at all, came with a long list of conditions.

My parents were divorced nine times between them before I was 21 years old. The first of these occurred when I was two. With each new step-parent that came into my life, a new set of emotions and conditions came with them. Sometimes it was sadness because I felt dismissed as an unimportant element in my parent's life every time a new person came into theirs. It seemed as if my parents loved me when they had no one else in their lives, but, as soon as there was, off to the sidelines I went! Often, I remember feeling as if I were invisible and wondered if I disappeared if anyone would notice or care.

By my teenage years, I had learned to be very self-critical. My love for myself depended on conditions. Conditions like how I looked, the grades I got, the friends I had, and the things I did. One of the biggest conditions was how much I weighed, and, at 15, I became a bulimic. I vomited or used laxatives at almost every meal for many years.

It never occurred to me that I might be hurting myself and could be doing serious damage to my body. All I could think about was "being perfect." If only I were skinnier, smarter, prettier, and better, then perhaps my dad would call or see me more often. If I were this or that, maybe the next time someone new came into one of my parents' lives, I wouldn't be forgotten.

I imagine we all have something in our history that made us feel as if we weren't loved at all, much less unconditionally. I remember hearing the term "unconditional love" as a kid and thinking, "That's just some feel-good term people use to make themselves feel better about love." In my child or teenage mind, I simply could not imagine how a person could give or receive love without conditions. Wasn't love all about conditions?

It took many years and a lot of therapy to realize that such a thing as unconditional love exists. That it is beautiful and amazing and more incredible than anything else we could ever know. And, sometimes, it begins within.

You have probably heard of The Golden Rule: "Do unto others as you would have others do unto you." A few years ago, while I was learning to love myself unconditionally, I thought of what I now call The Platinum Rule: "Do unto yourself as you would have others do unto you." After all, why would someone treat you well if you treat yourself badly?

So often people treat others better than they treat themselves. It's particularly common for women to be better to everyone else around them than they are to themselves. We sacrifice. For our husbands, our children, our friends, our jobs, and our community. Everything else becomes our priority, and we push ourselves further and further down the line.

During a therapy session, I realized I had been making other people's wellbeing a higher priority than my own. It suddenly became clear that I needed to take care of myself or I would be useless to others. I needed to treat myself with kindness and love, just like I wanted others to treat me. If I didn't think I was good enough to put first, why would anyone else?

At that point, my new project for unconditional self-love began. I started to look in the mirror and find at least one thing to compliment myself on every day. I would say things that maybe I didn't believe but hoped, if I said it enough, I eventually would. I started to write in a journal and would write all the positive qualities I thought I had. I started eating nutritional foods and exercising.

I read somewhere that the body is a temple and should be treated well and with respect. I hadn't been doing that. I was eating high-fat and sugary foods, and I wasn't exercising at all. So, I changed my diet and started running and lifting weights. I started to be grateful for all the good things in my life. I would thank God and the universe for giving me strength, resilience, and determination to get through all the tough times in my life. I began to look for ways where I had benefited because of the difficult times I had faced as a child. To my surprise, I found many.

After changing my perspective and looking for the good things that had come from my dysfunctional upbringing, I discovered I had developed emotional strength, tenacity, perseverance, determination, independence, and mental fortitude. All of the sudden, I was grateful and happy for my life experiences! I felt as if I could accomplish anything and make it through anything because I had made it through even tougher times before. Recognizing the shift in my thinking, I found a whole new world of possibilities in front of me, as opposed to the numerous road blocks and obstacles I used to see.

This new way of thinking empowered me, and I set goals for myself. Not long after, I was working as a secretary at a phone company and was turned down for a promotion. Worse still, I was asked to train the person who was hired. I remember thinking, "I wasn't good enough to do the job, but you want me to train the person you hired to do the job?" Before this change in consciousness, I would have gone into a downward spiral, feeling worthless, unimportant, and unvalued.

However, my thinking had changed, and I felt it was up to me to determine my value and worth. If this company didn't see me and my work as valuable, then I would find one that did. And, boy, did I!

Shortly after that incident, I left the phone company and became an assistant to a VP at another company. I was working with a sales team and saw people who were making ten, 20, and 30 thousand dollars a month. It wasn't long before I thought, "These people are making in a month what I make all year. I can see they aren't working harder than me, and I really don't think they're smarter than me. Even if they are, I can learn what they know."

And, that was it. I started looking for a job in sales and got one. It was hard work, and I had to learn a lot, but I did it. Just a few years later, I found myself the number one salesperson in my company and was making over a million dollars a year in commission. This all happened because I chose to change my thinking and to love myself unconditionally.

I applied this thinking to my personal and romantic life, also. For years, I had allowed myself to be treated badly by men. I found myself the "other woman" more than once. I had felt I wasn't good enough to have my own man, that I was only good enough to borrow one already taken. I also allowed men to show up late or not at all for dates and would go out with them the next time they asked anyway. Then, I read an amazing quote by Eleanor Roosevelt, "No one can take advantage of you without your permission."

This was a profound moment for me. It became clear that the reason men treated me badly was because I let them. Not just men but people in general. I had a habit of being a doormat for my friends and family as well. From that moment forward, I said, "No more." And, from that moment forward, I meant it. I chose to be the driving factor in my life and knew that if I wanted my life to change, *I* had to change.

I sat down and wrote a list of all the qualities I wanted in a husband. Then, I continued to write a list of all the things I wanted in every avenue of my life - work, home, education, travel, romantic, family, and more. I got a lot of criticism from others. "You're too picky," I was told early and often about what I wanted in a husband and life-long love partner. However, I felt I deserved all these qualities. I wasn't asking for more than I was willing to be or willing to give. It was up to me to be clear on who and what I wanted.

It took six years for me to find the partner I sought. Perhaps I could have found someone to spend my life with sooner, but, with every person I met, I felt I would be "settling" and wouldn't be happy over the long term. So, I stuck to my guns and remained single until I found the man that fit the bill. I'm so very glad I did! It took a long time, and, in those six years, I didn't have three dates with the same person. However, I promised myself I would not settle for less than

what I wanted in any area of my life. By keeping that promise ↳
myself, I was loving myself unconditionally.

Since making the conscious choice to love myself unconditionally
and get clear on all that I wanted, my life shifted 180 degrees. I
met and married the love of my life. I got my bachelor's degree in
communications and graduated magna cum laude. Though it took
me 13 years to finish college, I persevered until I achieved my goal.
I now write and speak for a living. Once upon a time, that was just a
dream. I help others accomplish what they want in life. That is a gift
I truly appreciate each and every day. I went from being a manicurist
to a millionaire by loving myself and being clear on what I wanted
and taking the actions necessary to make it happen.

Sometimes we look outside ourselves to be unconditionally loved.
I'm here to tell you it's up to each of us to do that for ourselves. As
the old Michael Jackson song reads, it starts "with the man in the
mirror." If you love yourself unconditionally, you will be fulfilled.
It's truly amazing how so often the universe reflects on the outside
what we are feeling on the inside. When you find the place in your
heart to love yourself unconditionally, you will find you start to
receive it!

Thoughts from Caroline

Animals provide an outlet for us to express love without the fear we might be tempted to allow in with a person. Because we feel completely and unconditionally accepted and loved by them, we can more easily provide them with the same love. We can appreciate their unconditionally giving natures, and, with conscious effort, attempt to emulate them. They help us, and we help them – a beautiful combination and another example for us to follow. Animals can teach us the most wondrous of lessons!

Affirmation

All experiences teach us love.

It was an exciting winter day in December when we finally decided to go and seek out a new canine edition to our family. Our children, Reiss and Phebe, who were five and four years old at the time, my husband, Jonathon, and I had decided it was time to bring a dog into our life! We had been searching in the local area for quite some time when we came across a woman who had wonderful, little puppies available. Bundled up in heavy winter coats, scarves, hats, and boots, we set off to go choose the newest edition to our family.

When we arrived, the woman had six puppies, but Jonathon and I decided we wanted a male so this narrowed our choices. She let the males run around, and one in particular kept coming and circling around my snow boots. He was only three pounds so he kept sliding on the melted snow on the tile floor. I picked him up and started cuddling him close, and my husband knew I had fallen in love already. We bundled him up in blankets for the cold, winter conditions outside.

On the trip home, Reiss and Phebe wanted to hold the little puppy and kept calling out different names from the back seat of the car. It was a running tradition within our extended family that the dogs' names began with a B so they were thinking of any word they could that started with a B. Jonathon called out Bugzee, and it immediately stuck. Bugzee was now the latest edition to our family, just in time to celebrate the Christmas holiday with us!

The following day, Jonathon had an appointment with the local vet to get Bugzee in for a checkup. He came through with flying colors, and we couldn't stop playing with him all the time!

Within a few days, though, Bugzee stopped eating and would barely drink his water. We contacted the woman we had received him from, she made a few suggestions, and then we took him back to the vet.

They gave him an IV and said he needed fluids but were not sure what was wrong with him. He came home the next day running around, seeming to be a bit more frisky, and then slowly started to go downhill again.

Our vets said they didn't know what to do, but that because of his small size we needed to get him to eat. I was not about to sit by and watch something so small, fragile, and innocent, who we had all just let into our hearts, literally fade away in front of my eyes!

I started calling other vets and clinics. We got him into another one, and they said they would run some tests but it would cost quite a bit of money. I talked it over with Jonathon and said if it were our kids, money would be no question, and we both had felt immediately as if Bugzee was another child to us. We told them to do what they had to do to find out what was wrong with our canine baby.

The next day we heard news we would never forget: Bugzee had pancreatitis and diabetes. The vet immediately suggested we put him to sleep. I started crying and said, "Absolutely not!" If it were one of our children, we wouldn't do that so why would we consider it for a canine child?

We took him home, and I started working on healing him with Reiki, crystals, sound vibrational healing, and anything I could think of! Jonathon sought out advice from alternative therapies and contacted more vets. We called every single vet we could find locally, and some not very close at all, and we finally found one that would at least take on Bugzee's case.

We took him in, and the vet technicians immediately fell in love with Bugzee, who could barely stand and just wanted to be cuddled in their arms. They set him up on a 24-hour watch with a technician we came to know very well over those next few weeks. With the right combination of medications and insulin injections, Bugzee's body bounced back, and he was ready to come home! It was a trying time, with money needed for both vet bills and holiday presents, but I insisted everything was going to be great, and we could work through anything together as a family.

Everyone was so excited to have Bugzee home for the holiday! He was running, happy, and a frisky little puppy. We celebrated Christmas together, and he came along with us to visit family and friends, who also had become very attached to him through this whole ordeal. We thought we had made it through and learned our lesson not to take even the simplest things for granted. It was one of the best holidays we had ever had together as a family.

Soon after, however, Bugzee's health went down again. He wouldn't eat and was losing weight again, and at only three pounds when we got him not even four weeks prior, he couldn't afford to lose any more. He started vomiting and was very weak. We rushed him to the emergency vet who stabilized him with IV's and medicine until we could get him back to his regular vet.

That day was one we will never forget. The doctors came in and said they had done everything they knew but couldn't stabilize him, as he was getting too weak and losing too much weight. They had no suggestions, and we knew we were going to lose him. We took Bugzee home with us, cuddled up in his special blanket, so our children, family, and friends could say one last goodbye.

Jonathon and I knew we did not want him to suffer and that we couldn't help him any more than we had already. We had given him unconditional love, as he did for us, and he had given us a special area in our hearts that we would never forget. We said our heartbreaking goodbyes, had our children stay with their grandparents, and went back to the vet.

When we arrived, the vet technician that had been taking care of Bugzee asked if she could be there when we put him down. They had a little room set up for things like this, and Bugzee had touched so many hearts at this clinic that many of their staff wanted to say goodbye.

I will never forget that heartbreaking day in January. As he was sitting on the table curled up in my arms, I gave him one last kiss on the head and said, "I will see you again soon," as he closed his eyes and his body went limp. Jonathon started crying so deeply that I had to hold Bugzee and let his spirit go to a better place.

My husband and I had other animals at many times but never really understood until Bugzee what degree of unconditional love could come into our lives from a loved pet. Animals have huge hearts, loving spirits, and truly show this in every possible way from the moment they enter our lives. Our own hearts and spirits make room for these wonderful, loving spirits, and this changes everything!

We learned many lessons over that time period that changed our entire family. If it were not for Bugzee in our life, we wouldn't see the wonders we now have with the four canine companions we've rescued. We are now able to provide them with the unconditional love he taught all of us.

The one month Bugzee was with us created a portal for appreciation, gratitude, and unconditional love for all living spirits – especially those who touch our hearts in unique ways, such as the little, innocent canine companion who had a strong fight for life and a huge heart of gold that could cross any boundary in the world!

Thoughts from Caroline

If God deems us worthy of absolute love, who are we to doubt our lovability? If God has deemed our neighbors and our friends and even our enemies as worthy of absolute love, who are we to doubt their lovability? What better example do we have for how to love than God? If we believe God loves us absolutely, then we should choose to love ourselves absolutely. If we believe God loves others absolutely, then we should choose also to love them absolutely. We may want to complicate the matter of love, but God's love is simple, and so can be ours.

Affirmation

I embrace absolute love.

Rick Lannoye

teacher, philosopher, and author of "Hell? No!"

For people of the Christian faith, one of the biggest questions in life is the nature of God's love. There are those who say God's love is limited, that as much as He might love the entire world right now, there will eventually come a day when He will give up on some of us in the name of "justice" or "punishment." Others say God loves all of us *unconditionally*, that He never gives up on us and, despite our many mistakes, always responds to us with love. Whichever answer a Christian embraces, every relationship he or she has will be deeply influenced by it.

About 20 years ago, I found myself pondering the nature of God's love in an attempt to figure out which view was "right." I'd converted to Christian Evangelicalism as a young teen and, initially, found myself basking in the knowledge that *nothing* could separate me from the love of God. Over time, however, I heard a different story, that there was another side to God, a side that knew nothing of forgiveness and demanded revenge.

In my heart, I strongly sensed this could not be, that God could not be vindictive or vengeful, but was instead loving and kind. It felt to me that if God would demand retribution, then forgiveness could not exist. In turn, unconditional love, which is directly dependent on forgiveness, would be impossible. I asked myself: If our greatest moral example wants to get back at those who offend Him, how can we do any better?

For clarity, I turned to Jesus, who, with the words he said and the life he lived, proved to me that God's love knows no bounds, has no restrictions, and comes without conditions, that God *never* gives up on us and, despite our many mistakes, *always* responds to us with love. The teachings of Jesus made it clear to me that God's love is unequivocally unconditional.

For example, in Exodus 21:24, Moses says, "If you gouge out someone's eye, then you should have your eye gouged out." We are told Moses was speaking directly on God's behalf. But, during Jesus' famous Sermon on the Mount, he quotes this passage and then adds, "But I say, if any should strike you on the cheek, turn to him the other." Jesus also taught we are to return love for hate and good for evil in order "to be children of the Father in Heaven … who sends the rain to both good and bad people."

Jesus saw the Old Testament laws, not as the final and full revelation of what God was really like, but as God's plan to deter the worst of human behavior until we were ready to hear His true message. He explained that Moses gave laws "because of the hardness of men's hearts." According to Jesus, God's ultimate desire is to completely put an end to the pain and suffering humans cause one another.

All through the gospels, one can see how Jesus' revolutionary message was difficult for people to grasp, even his closest disciples. In Matthew 18:21-22, Peter asks Jesus, "Lord, how many times should I forgive my brother after he sins against me? Seven times?" Peter likely thought he had misunderstood Jesus, that Jesus was saying we should give people a few chances, but eventually there would come a point of judgment. But, Jesus reiterated, "No, but seventy times seven!"

Ultimately, it was Jesus' death on the cross that served as the greatest demonstration of how unconditional God's love is. If ever there was a time when God would have lost his patience and given up on humanity, it would have been during Jesus' passion. Like the prophet Isaiah said, he took on the worst of human transgressions but at no point did he give any indication that he wanted "satisfaction" or "justice" or "revenge." On the contrary, Jesus' unconditional love was proven beyond all doubt when he looked upon the very people who had tortured and were killing him and said, "Father, forgive them, for they know not what they do."

Faith in God's limitless love changes how we treat ourselves and everyone else - our spouse, our children, our friends, our neighbors, even people on the other side of the globe - and leads us toward lasting and peaceful relationships. When others let us down, we are reminded of God's patience and infinite forgiveness. It is precisely at these times of such disappointment that we're instructed to be mindful of how God is patient and forgiving toward us, thus Jesus' instruction to pray, "Forgive us our trespasses as we forgive those who trespass against us." We remember that we, too, are called upon to be ever patient and forgiving toward others.

Unconditional love and limitless forgiveness go hand-in-hand. Only when the cycle of revenge is broken by forgiveness can we know lasting love and peace. Unconditional love and forgiveness serve as the springboard from which we come to believe in ourselves and to accept that we are all worth something. It's no accident that many of the worst atrocities committed are by those who never had anyone who believed in them.

Jesus had a new solution to this cycle. Jesus preached that we can stop the hurt of others by being the first to forgive. It is a courageous stance to take and is, for all practical purposes, the only real way to reduce the human suffering caused by other humans.

Whether we're talking about Middle East conflicts, troubles with a "rebellious" teenager, or an argument with a spouse, the path toward real peace lies, not in making sure all hurts caused are repaid in kind, but by being the first to bravely proclaim, "I'm stopping this vicious cycle to go a better way. I'm going to forgive and not give up. I'm embracing the way of unconditional love. I will love like God."

Thoughts from Caroline

Fear is perhaps the greatest obstacle to unconditional love. We can release fears when we understand that love is always greater than any fear. Each time we discover a fear, we can acknowledge it and choose to walk through it. This renders the fear powerless and restores the natural power of our souls. We are also able to step further into the flow of the universe, where we will feel rewarded for our bravery, as the flow of the universe feels safe and peaceful and easy.

Affirmation

Love is always stronger than my fears.

Katharine C. McCorkle, Ph.D

founder and CEO of Balanced Heart™ Healing Center, a non-profit integrative health center for mind, body, and spirit

"Your task is not to seek for love, but merely to seek and find all the barriers within yourself that you have built against it." ~ Rumi

I am not fond of snakes. Years ago, I loved to backpack in the Sierra Nevada mountains of California. Others had told me of a magical place: a remote and very beautiful area surrounding a lake. I decided to make a circular backpacking trip to the area. I knew I would have to pass through a valley that was heavily populated with rattlesnakes, but I decided to make the trip anyway ... alone.

I made the trip as a solo retreat to discover myself in relationship with the mountains and their mysteries. I arrived at the rattlesnake valley around noon on the second day and was startled by what I saw. Even though I had known to expect rattlesnakes, and brought shin guards to protect myself, I was totally unprepared for the visceral terror I experienced at seeing so many snakes so densely packed together throughout the valley.

They lounged on every rock and blended in with the thick, scrubby vegetation. I could barely take a step on the path without danger of inadvertently stepping on one. Without the snakes, it wouldn't take long to move through that valley, and, with them, I didn't know if I could make it at all!

I paused at the entrance to the rattlesnake valley and considered the possibility I might die of a snake-bite alone in the wilderness. I thought about turning back without completing my trip. Something in me wouldn't allow that, however. Perhaps I wanted to prove something to myself. Perhaps I was determined to get to the lake (this was the only path.) Perhaps I just knew from someplace deep inside myself that if only I could be at peace, I would not give off the scent of fear and arouse the rattlers to action.

It was around noon, the hottest part of the day in that high mountain valley, and the rattlesnakes were taking their siestas. I silently donned my shin guards and took a few moments to quiet myself inside. I imagined myself in the snakes' position and gave them time to accept my presence in their space. I blessed them and asked for a peaceful passage through their valley. Then, slowly, carefully paying attention to where I placed my foot at every step, I began the journey.

I wondered if the snakes could hear my heart pounding out of my chest or feel the vibration of my energy around them. I certainly felt theirs! With each step I took, my peace and confidence about my survival grew. I found a pace and rhythm at which I could move without disturbing either myself or them. I found my balance among the rattlesnakes. Harmony ruled the earth in that place.

Decades later, I decided to move my psychology practice into an empty space in my home. At the time, I performed many custody evaluations, and my colleagues thought I was out of my mind to bring that contentious energy into my home. They also had concerns about my safety because my home is in the woods, at the end of a street. Because I respected them, I took their concerns seriously, but their views didn't resonate in my spirit.

My thought was to create a beautiful, holistic healing environment so soothing that by the time my clients walked the gently winding path from the road through the woods to my office, half of my job would be already done. I thought that would prevent any trouble from coming to me - and it did. In the end, I was simply unwilling to live my life in fear of what might happen!

What is perfect love? How do we receive it and offer it to others? Shortly after moving my office into my home, I was out in my "summer office," a beautiful space between the pond and the swimming pool where I sink into communion with all of life. The tall oak trees form a protective bowl around my home and backyard, and I am transported to a higher place as I become one with the treetops swaying gently in the breeze as the hawks circle overhead. Frogs punctuate my most momentous thoughts with their intermittent croaking. Hummingbirds, dragonflies, and all manner of butterflies grace the space with their playful presence.

Like a gift from God, a surprising thing happened that hot August afternoon in 2002, as I was enjoying my backyard Garden of Eden. Ten principles for living unconditional love emerged fully formed into my heart and mind! In that moment, I realized I must learn to live the "10 Principles" consistently in my own life before I could teach them to others.

The 10 Principles:

1. Open your heart and trust.
2. Give and receive without attachment to the outcome.
3. Create safety for yourself and others.
4. Welcome everything as a blessing … especially when it doesn't look like one!
5. See only goodness (Love.)
6. DREAM BIG!!!
7. Take responsibility for everything … NO exceptions.
8. Let go of what no longer serves you.
9. Have no judgments so truth can be revealed.
10. BE the miracle you wish to create.

These ten principles are simple but definitely not easy to live all the time! At first, I didn't realize that opening my heart and trusting meant learning to trust myself and letting go of the self-doubt that had been my constant companion for much of my life. I realized very quickly how attached I was to my desire to have things my own way, my need to be "right," and my need for the approval of others, without which I was unable to believe in myself. I also realized when I didn't create safety for others, they distanced themselves from me, and then I no longer felt safe.

Learning to see only goodness and love was a challenge because I still carried many wounds from earlier in my life. Fears of being hurt, rejected, or abandoned clouded my perceptions of many people and relationships, including the relationship with myself! At moments when I was able to get over my fears of being not good enough or undeserving and take a step (or sometimes a leap) outside my comfort zone, I became fearless, and dreaming big was easy. It was then that my passion soared, I stepped into the "flow," and began seriously living my life.

Nonetheless, taking responsibility for everything is not an easy thing to do! It can feel overwhelming, a "balance challenge" in disguise. When things didn't work out the way I hoped they would, I had to go looking for how I created those outcomes, too, and that often led to painful self-awareness and a deep need for self-forgiveness.

The necessity of forgiving ourselves is the price we pay for deeper self-awareness of who we've been in the past. Forgiveness is the willingness to let go, to recognize that I was doing the best I could at the time, and that, if I could have done better, I would have. Isn't that true for everyone all the time?

Self-forgiveness freed me to feel "good enough" and deserving of my dreams, despite my imperfections. It freed me to give myself a new beginning any time I wanted one, and I was willing to let go of the past in order to receive it. My passion soared!

Judgments always pull us out of balance by forcing a choice and may lead to regrets about what we let go. The challenge is to recognize that when we judge others, we're also judging ourselves and separating ourselves from the goodness that is available in our relationships. When we judge ourselves, we limit our capacity to share our God-given gifts with the world.

Being the miracle is stepping into the "flow" of life and living in grace. Those moments began to come more frequently and brought with them the opportunity to notice how I was creating them. Hallelujah! The good news is that the better I got at living the 10 Principles, the faster everyone around me seemed to improve.

In my psychology practice, I had always treated people unconditionally, regardless of their insurance status or ability to pay for services. I trusted that God was bringing me the people who could benefit from my help, and my job was to help them.

There's an aphorism in the mental health field that you can only take your client as far as you yourself have gone. It was so much easier to love my clients than it was to love myself. But if I didn't deeply love myself, how could I teach them to love themselves, too? Interestingly, as I learned to love myself more unconditionally, I noticed that my clients were getting better faster!

Recently, I was escorting a new client out of my office when we were startled to see in the center of my waiting room floor a young snake looking up at me, as if he were waiting for his own appointment to begin. My client jumped back in fright, and I gently and firmly ushered the snake out the door, thereby restoring a sense of safety and balance to all.

Fear is the doorway to all our dreams coming true! As my clients and I say "no" to fear, it opens the way to an expanded awareness of ourselves and the infinite possibilities in every moment. Saying "no" to fear shouts "YES!" to life. Fear is merely a lie and an illusion, a masquerade that limits our choices. Denying fear a place in our life frees us to act out of unconditional love instead. As we become grateful to fear for inviting us into that glorious new place, we heal and forgive whatever has held us back in the past, and grow toward living love now and forever more.

Thoughts from Caroline

Family bonds often provide our strongest examples of unconditional love. When we are blessed with this in our lives, it gives us confidence in our own pursuits and the ability to pass this example of unconditional love on to further generations. Even through difficult times, the underlying love remains, and we can always choose to focus on the strengths of the unconditional love we have received and given.

Affirmation

I choose to see my family relationships as

opportunities to create love.

Love Like God
Shirley W. Mitchell
author of six books, including "Fabulous after 50®: Finding Fulfillment for Tomorrow," and owner-celebrity talk show host of the syndicated media group, "Aging Outside the Box®"

When my beautiful, Godly mother passed through the pearly gates of heaven and danced in her golden shoes with my father on the streets of gold, I wrote her a love letter in which I thanked her for giving me unconditional love.

Dear Mother,
You taught me how to love without conditions. When I was a little girl, you made me feel I was special. You treated me like a princess. That special feeling gave me self-confidence, balance in my life, and courage to live life with a positive attitude. You gave me wings to fly throughout life with an optimistic view. You have the most caring, giving spirit of any person I have met in my life. Giving was so prominent to your personality; you did not realize that you were selfless.
I Love You,
Shirley

Mothers have a unique and crucial role to fill in the lives of their children. The unconditional love, care, nurturance, and encouragement a mother gives to her child never ceases. The fabulous singer Sandi Patti, when interviewed by Christian Life Magazine, said, "My highest note in life is motherhood!"

Ninety percent of women are mothers. I would bet that most of those mothers love their children unconditionally. They see possibilities, potential, and hope in their children. Many have a God-given ability to create an atmosphere conducive to the production of mature, well-adjusted adults.

A mother's love for her newborn baby may be the paradigm of

unconditional love or real love. Unconditional love of mother
and child creates a relationship that is binding through eternity.
Unconditional love leaves footprints on one's heart.

While motherhood may be the most important job in the universe,
fathers also fill a special role in their children's lives. My tall,
handsome, Godly father was a man of true, pure integrity and an
excellent cotton farmer. Back in the 1950s, all of my family - brother,
sister, aunts, uncles, cousins, grandfather, and grandmother - worked
the cotton fields for our livelihood, and most of our living was
maintained on a 60-acre farm. We grew the majority of our food,
such as vegetables and fruit trees, and we raised cows, chickens, and
pigs.

The whole Todd family worked on the farm from daylight until
dark. It was hard, dirty work, but we had perks. On the top terrace
row of the 30-acre cotton patch, my dad planted a very long row of
watermelons. At break time, when the sun bore down hard and we
all glistened with sweat, my father would blow his whistle. Then,
we each took a watermelon and sat on the ground under the shade of
the old oak trees that lined the field. We would eat watermelon, sing
songs, and tell stories. At the end of the day, the young folks would
climb upon the top of the picked cotton as the sun set in the west,
while my dad drove the loaded truck through the fields to our three
small houses, which lined a dirt road.

We didn't have much money, and my parents made every penny
count. But, through some miracle that could only be divine
providence brought to life by parents who dreamed and planned to
make it happen, we had enough for me to own an upright piano and
take piano lessons. Each Saturday morning, I joyfully walked the two
miles to my piano lessons. It was the highlight of my week.

One morning, my father was moving my precious piano to our new
home a few yards from my grandparents' house when the tractor hit a
huge root of an old oak tree and dislodged the piano. I watched as the
massive, wooden piano bounced out to the hard ground, rolled over
and over, and broke into a thousand splinters.

I was devastated. The magnitude of loss sank deep into my soul. I ran, screamed, and cried. My father caught me, picked me up in his strong arms and hugged me to him as I beat upon his muscular shoulders with my small, clenched fists. "You broke my piano!" I screamed into his ear.

He held my trembling body until I stopped sobbing. Then his big, green eyes looked deeply into my bewildered, dark brown ones. His face was sad, and he said, "Before I die, I will buy you a new piano."

A decade went by, and then another. I grew up, got married, and moved to a new home with my husband and children. One day the doorbell rang. A piano salesman introduced himself. "Your dad has paid for any one you would like," he said, and he handed me a catalogue filled with pages and pages of beautiful pianos. Through my tears, I selected my favorite.

To this day, my piano is a source of great joy. I love playing it! My children learned to play on it, and now my grandchildren touch the ivory keys as well. The piano occupies a special place in my living room and a special place in my heart, along with my father.

My father worked every day of his life to provide for his family and often took on extra shifts at night in the cotton mills to give us the things we wanted. When I was a senior in high school, I had the chance to go on the first senior trip my high school had ever taken. It was to Washington, D.C. I was so excited, but I didn't think there was any way we could afford for me to go. My father worked day and night for months. I will never forget the day I stood in our small kitchen, and he handed me a check for $360 and took me in his strong, farmer-tanned arms and hugged me in a giant bear hug.

Through his unconditional love and self-sacrifice, my father gave me the chance to take my first trip by train outside the state of Alabama and experience the excitement of Washington, D.C. with my classmates. Fifty-four years later, I still get a thrill out of visiting Washington, D.C. His was the kind of true love that can last a lifetime, give happiness, and make his children whole.

My father's love empowered me to become the woman I am today. My three wonderful children have given me ten grandchildren and one great-grandchild. This, plus my career as an author, speaker, columnist, and internet-radio talk show host, fills my emotional tank.

Grandparents also play a large role in teaching unconditional love to their grandchildren. My Mama Todd and Paw Paw Todd were the grandparents who worked the cotton fields with me when I was growing up. My Mama Todd had arthritis in her knees and was unable to kneel down and pick cotton on her knees to relieve her back. Consequently, she bent from her waist to pick cotton and had to drag her pick sack behind her all day.

When I felt down or tired, she would keep my spirits up and motivate me by saying, "Let's have a race! The one that picks the most pounds of cotton gives the other one a dollar!" Our poundage at the end of the day would be pretty close, but she always made sure I won. Even though she was tired and hurt all over, she would often sneak handfuls of cotton into my pick sack just to be sure. By caring more about my happiness than her own, my grandmother taught me a valuable lesson in unconditional love.

I attribute Paw Paw with my love for music. He was a stutterer, but when he sang, his stutter would disappear. With his beautiful voice and knowledge of music, he spent many hours directing the church choir and drama productions. My Paw Paw's best friend was a concert pianist. Together, the two men taught me to sing, gave me encouragement, and supported me while I performed. My Paw Paw, through his unconditional love, took the time and patience to keep me involved in his musical life. As Thomas Carlyle said, "Music is well said to be the speech of angels."

Now that I am a grandmother, I understand the phrase, "Grandchildren are a caress from God." My oldest granddaughter is getting married so my blood line of unconditional love will go on. My youngest granddaughter, a three-year-old, adopted Chinese girl, is enveloped in unconditional love from my daughter and her husband, who adore her.

I see the sparks of unconditional love passing down through the generations of my family; I see them create a fire of true love. God is Love. The love of God is an oasis of peace surrounded by the sands of time, and our families are but a part of it.

Thoughts from Caroline

Our thoughts about ourselves control the reality we experience and color everything we see, hear, and feel. We can choose positive thoughts, we can choose supportive thoughts, and we can choose loving thoughts. Recognizing the sanctity of our soul helps. Recognizing we wouldn't criticize a friend the way we criticize ourselves helps. Recognizing that the approval we most need in the world is our own is life-changing.

Affirmation

" I deserve my own love. "

Love Like God

Kristen Moeller

bestselling author of "Waiting for Jack: Confessions of a Self-Help Junkie
– How to Stop Waiting and Start Living Your Life" and creator of
"Author Your Brilliance™"

Something catches my eye as I sit down to write - a golden Aspen leaf floating by my window. Having completed its life cycle, it now freely follows the fall breeze on its way to transform to something else. Does the leaf struggle with accepting itself and its fate? I don't believe so. Why are we humans so critical of our cycles in life? What if we could embrace all that it means to be human?

True unconditional love would be welcoming the extraordinary and the mundane, the views from soaring heights as well as the smell of the gutter, the glory of success and terror of failure, as well as everything in between. My wish for humanity is that we could be even just a smidge more self-accepting - beginning with ourselves and extending to all we encounter. That leaf certainly isn't making itself wrong for its imminent decay.

Each fall, I reminisce about my life prior to entering recovery in 1989. I was severely bulimic, engaged in a slow, crushing descent into an addictive cycle that would stoke my fears and send me seeking food, drugs, and booze to quell those fears.

How did I end up with such self-loathing? How did I miss what was really there? How did I not see? As a teenager, all I saw was wrong: my feet were too big, legs too short, nose too large, lips too small ... and my stomach - well, it was "supposed" to be flat as a board.

Illogically, dieting seemed like a good idea, but on my already slim frame, losing even five pounds was immediately noticeable. My flesh started to melt away, and people commented. Did I connect the dots? No. By losing weight, I received the attention I sought. Sure, the attention was out of concern, but I missed that part. Instead, it filled a bizarre craving, concealed even from myself.

I couldn't see the big picture. I made decisions from a place of emptiness and lack. If I had been granted a glimpse into the future and foresaw spending the next seven years of my life at the mercy of a devastating eating disorder, perhaps I might have chosen something else.

Challenged throughout high school, college brought a whole new level of demands. I lost my way even more. My inability to stop binging and purging left me bewildered and afraid. I knew I was missing life - as in *real* life. A life beyond ravenous eating and hunting for a safe place to purge, often in the dark of night. A life like my fellow students seemed to have: time spent in the beautiful Colorado wilderness - camping trips, biking, hiking. Smiling faces, so healthy and happy. Or perhaps, even time spent figuring out what I wanted to be when I graduated. I desperately longed for something else, but I was trapped.

It wasn't that I didn't try to stop. Each day, I would promise myself I wouldn't engage in my demoralizing bulimic behavior. And, each day, I would fail. At one point of desperation, I reached out for help from my parents and saw a therapist weekly from then on. She tried her best to help me. We talked about my feelings and my past, experimented with various anti-depressants ... maybe it kept me alive, but I still couldn't break the habit.

A 30-day stay at a treatment center during the summer of my junior year helped. Suddenly I had a brief flicker of understanding about my behavior. I learned that "fat" wasn't a feeling. This was news to me! I learned about assertiveness and using "I statements" to communicate my needs. Yet, I returned to college without an adequate support structure and quickly slid back into my old behavior.

Two years later, graduation was right around the corner, looming like an ominous black cloud. My friends were headed off to careers or graduate school. I had no idea what I could ever do or be. Fortunately, my parents stepped in again and found me another treatment center.

This time felt different. I was miserable and finally willing to try anything. A faint glimmer of hope kept me going. Maybe, just maybe, my life could be different. The terror I felt the last night before going to rehab was almost unbearable. The end was in sight; something had to change.

And, it did. I was given the gift of desperation and threw myself into recovery with all the eagerness that only those who have been given a second chance at life understand.

First, I learned to accept and, then later, to love myself. I began to understand the many factors along the way that formed who I had become. My parents divorced when I was young, and the resulting moves back and forth between them brought the issues of adjusting to new schools and trying to fit in. All I wanted to do was belong, but every time, my shyness would take over. And, much to my dismay, I never seemed to wear the "right" clothes.

I would try to prepare and anticipate how people would dress at my new school, but somehow each time I missed – wearing tight designer jeans when "they" were wearing preppy chinos, wearing the *wrong* shoes. ("Tacky," they said.) Then, there was the tragic death of my aunt, who was killed on a motorcycle, my mom's alcoholism, my own discovery of alcohol and drugs, and more divorce. Life mostly seemed sad and out of control.

Anna Freud wrote, "I was always looking outside myself for strength and confidence, but it comes from within. It is there all the time." The adventure since that day I said, "Yes!" to recovery has been about my realization of this in *all* areas of my life.

All those early questions I asked and decisions I made - I finally saw the answers. Am I enough? Of course. Is there enough love to go around? Yes, more than enough. Does my parents' divorce mean anything about me? Not at all. Do I need to prove how good I am? Not in the least bit. Do I have to be sick to get attention? No, I can just ask for what I need. What happens if someone thinks my shoes are tacky? Nothing! It doesn't mean anything about me!

Today my life is about the journey. Sure, I have my bumps in the road. Sometimes more than I would like! I have dealt with cancer, death of beloved friends, fertility struggles, and pregnancy losses, but I have never gone back to my eating disorder or addictions. I find the more exigent opportunities to be the daily ups and downs of life. That's where the real test of unconditional love comes into play.

I have committed my life to personal growth, transformation, and helping others become free from what stops them. And, sometimes I don't "wanna!" Sometimes I would rather stay in my pajamas, curl up in a ball, and quit than go out and lead a workshop or speak on stage. Sometimes my self-doubt screams so loudly I am surprised my neighbors don't complain.

And, now I return to that leaf blowing by my window in its natural cycle of life. Does loving ourselves unconditionally mean we are supposed to feel empowered and strong *all* the time? Or, is it perhaps natural to have our own cycles?

For most of 2007, I was growing and expanding, then I hit a plateau. It was actually more of a colossal wall. I was dismayed! I had hoped that by "this" time in my life, I wouldn't find myself in such confusion again! In one rich, poignant moment, I questioned myself and my life. What was I doing? Where was I going? Why was I still searching? What was I waiting for? Would I ever let myself be?

An Oliver Wendell Holmes quote ran through my mind, "Many people die with their music still inside them." Then, out of the blue, I had a flash of inspiration - I would write a book. I would explore this topic! I would discover why so many of us wait and don't live fully, why we are so hard on ourselves, why we never seem to break free from this cycle.

However, there was a slight dilemma: I was *not* a writer. I didn't consider myself to be someone who expressed well on paper. Fortunately, I knew my inspiration was noble, and I knew how to take action - to move forward even when every molecule in my body told me to stop. I knew I could "feel the fear and do it anyway." Yet, here I was at another turning point. I had to transform my view of myself once again. The only way I could do this was to write.

Some days I cried and wanted to give up; others I celebrated my courage. I wrote, re-wrote, ripped it all up, burned what was left, and started over. I hired editors, changed directions, then changed back. I danced in the moonlight and curled up in a ball on the floor. I told everyone I was writing and then wished I hadn't. I grew, contracted, then grew again, stretching further than I ever thought possible.

A mere three years after that inspiration, my book became a bestseller. Reviews from previously unknown readers poured in - thanking me for my message and telling me I had written their words and expressed their hearts and hurts. They tell me I have given them encouragement and inspiration. They know I am a fellow traveler.

You see, I know what it's like to hit the wall of doubt and fear. I know the discomfort, the pain, and now I also know the joy and the exhilaration of breaking free from constraints. And, most importantly, I have come to know that unconditional love is not an arrival point.

Unconditional love is just that - love *without* conditions. It's to love ourselves, even when we fail, when we hurt, when we are joyful, when we struggle, when we are cruel, when we are kind, when we are at the top, when we are in the gutter. It's to love ourselves *even* when we don't love ourselves. It's to be in the cycle of life, just like the leaves that fall every year outside my window.

Thoughts from Caroline

No matter how much pain we have experienced in our lives, we can choose to release it. No matter what wrongs we have perceived ourselves to have committed, we can choose to release them. We can choose to release all illusions that we are anything less than a perfect soul from God. If we reach a dark night of our soul, we can rejoice, for we know the dawn will bring with it a promise of rebirth. All is well in God's world.

Affirmation

I release my chains of bondage and find peace in my own heart.

Roy Nelson

spiritual healer who helps others address and heal the underlying causes of addictions so they can be happy, healthy, and free

Where I came from, there was no such thing as self-love. I grew up in poverty as one of four children in a small town in Texas. My father was sadistically violent with our family and was known in the town as a drunk. On account of many evictions, my family moved often.

At one time, for three years, my entire family, including my grandmother, lived in a two-room tin house. At school and at home, I experienced and lived with the constant threat of physical violence. And, I was no stranger to emotional and sexual abuse. Though the idea of God and church might have brought me comfort, my experience of "hell, fire, and brimstone" religion brought only further terror and alienation to my life.

I worked to make money from a very young age, and at the age of 14, I left home and school permanently to pursue a work opportunity in another town. At 17, I joined the Army, where I served in Korea, Germany, Saudi Arabia, and the United States. By the age of 20, I had married a woman who had a daughter, and a year later she gave birth to our son. Nine months after that, she gave birth to twin boys. By the very young age of 22, I had transitioned from a harsh childhood to being responsible for providing for a wife and four children! The emotional repercussions took their toll.

I had battled my weight throughout my life. I was heavy as a child, and by the time I was in my early twenties, I weighed 230 pounds. When, after seven years in the Army, I began a career in sales and marketing, my success was evident – and matched only by my progressive weight gain. I also drank heavily. In general, my lifestyle was chaotic, and I was spinning out of control.

By my late twenties, I was suffering from panic attacks and phobias, and I was seeking help through a variety of mental health practitioners: psychiatrists, psychologists, and medical hypno-analysts. Nothing I tried stopped the madness. At age 32, I was 275 pounds, and while I was experiencing outer success, I was an emotional wreck inside. I hated my self, my thoughts, and my actions. I believed I was the worst person in the world and didn't deserve any hope of forgiveness.

Late one night, when all my "painkillers" had failed to keep the guilt, remorse, fear, and despair at bay, I crawled out of my bed and, on my knees, cried out for help from a God I thought I didn't believe in. I asked for forgiveness for my contemptuous attitude toward Him and for all the things I had done, thought, and said that had caused me so much shame and guilt.

God must have been waiting.

In that moment, I felt a peace come over me. My angst lifted, and I was able to get back into bed and fall asleep peacefully. When I awoke the next day, I was amazed at my ever-growing sense of peace. I felt free for the first time in years!

The grace I experienced that night enabled me to feel valued and loved enough to stop punishing myself with addictions. I felt worthy of a better life. I began to lose weight effortlessly, and I no longer drank alcohol.

My whole life changed. I continually sought more of the peace I found that night, and, over of a period of about nine months, I shed 100 pounds. I ended behaviors that had caused me guilt and self-loathing, and I started new disciplines of self-care that made me feel better about myself every day.

In my efforts to find answers in the inner pain I had suffered throughout my life, I talked to others who had struggled with addictions, as well as spiritual and medical figures who strived to understand the workings of the subconscious mind. As I put the pieces of the puzzle together, my recovery grew stronger, and I wanted to stop more than just my major addictions. I continued on to the lesser ones. I had a burning desire to BE TOTALLY FREE. And that desire drove me to break through the bondage of all my addictions - and even from the addictive personality itself! I knew God would give me the strength to accomplish my goals.

It is through love that we are healed. After "cracking the code" of my own problems over 34 years ago, I turned to help others do the same. There were many spiritual elements to the transformation I experienced: surrender to a higher power, prayer, humility, and forgiveness. However, the thing that was most responsible for bringing me peace, joy, and – most importantly - self-love, was my devotion to helping others heal.

The nature of the addict's mind is self-obsession. There is very little room for thoughts of God or others when we focus on our selves, our lives, our worries, and our fears. We feel guilty and unworthy of the good things that happen, and we block ourselves off from the abundance all around.

My goal is to help others come to love themselves so that they no longer have to punish themselves with food, alcohol, pills, or other forms of self-abuse. When I turn my mind to those who are hurting and need guidance to recreate their lives, I forget about myself and become a channel for God's love. This creates an expansive feeling of love and oneness inside of me, which allows me to say yes to all of God's gifts. Through His love, I can heal others. I feel grateful, useful, and whole, which is the best description of self-love I know.

Since my own healing, it has been my life's mission to help others heal themselves with the help of God. There is nothing more important in my life. I have been very blessed to be able to touch the hearts and lives of many people who were once suffering but now are free.

I believe that because God and others have so generously been there for me, I provide an example for others. And, it is my privilege to be that example. Because I have suffered at such a deep level, and been healed, I want to be there for those who are suffering and seek healing. I *know* that love heals, and we all can be free.

Thoughts from Caroline

How many times have we claimed to love God unconditionally and then stood by as a neighbor struggled, or as a friend spiraled, or even distanced ourselves when a relative simply "got on our nerves?" We cannot love God unconditionally without loving everyone and everything unconditionally. We are all part of the same spiritual family, even those on the other side of the world whom we will never meet. Recognizing that we are all parts of a whole, and that we, ourselves, are a valued part of that whole, will reunite us together as one.

I focus on extending unconditional love to all,

including those who are hardest for me.

Paramahamsa Nithyananda

the "ever-smiling swami," a young, enlightened master of Yoga and meditation who has inspired more than four million followers worldwide

A young sannyasi (spiritual aspirant) once sought out an enlightened master and asked him, "O spiritual teacher, I want to learn how to love God with all my heart! I have practiced yoga and meditation, I have left home and lived as a wandering monk, I have done all possible austerities, but somehow I am unable to experience the love for the Divine which the great saints sing about!"

The spiritual teacher looked at the man compassionately and asked him, "Have you ever loved a woman with all your heart?"

"Of course not!" said the young man, "I have dedicated my life to God!"

"Then go," said the spiritual teacher, "Go and first love a woman, or your parents, or a friend with all your being – and then come back to learn how to love God!"

Understand, it is easy to feel (or think we feel) unconditional love for God or a spiritual teacher. The tough part is feeling the same love for your neighbor!

I always tell people: If you can feel the same love you feel toward me toward others, also, then you have caught the thread of real love; you have started feeling Existence in everything. Slowly, you will move on to embracing everything and everyone as part of Existence where all love becomes unconditional.

Unconditional love is something so deep, so energizing, that you will not know it unless you experience it. Love is an expression of energy, not something that is transferred from one being to another. Love is not a course taught in school. How do I know this? Let me ask you this: Can you love people when you meet them for the first time?

You probably think, no, how can I love someone I do not know or just met? So let me tell you, with a little bit of intellectual understanding and meditation, you will realize that you can love anyone without a reason, without a cause. You can love the trees on the road; you can caress them and feel the energy flow from you. You can love people whom you pass by on the road without even knowing them. Love is actually your very being, not a distilled quality you possess that can be handed out willy-nilly.

I was recently put in jail for 53 days while I was investigated for a crime I did not commit. At my bail hearing, the judge released me and said, "There is no evidence, no victim, and no witness."

In those 53 days, I did not have a bed, just the concrete floor of my cell to sleep on. The cell floor was washed with cold water just before I was to go to sleep. Loud music was played all night, and bright lights were left on.

This whole event increased the intense energy in my body of unconditional love and compassion for the people who are in so much pain that they do these things. I experienced a whole new unconditional love expressing though my body. I do not have to think about these things as thoughts to invoke them, my enlightened state expresses without any thought. That is the beauty of enlightenment. I don't have to think loving thoughts to feel love. Love is constantly expressing. When a situation occurs that is aggressive or violent, my being knows there is much pain in the person who is taking the actions, and I respond in a variety of ways, with the core quality being unconditional love. It is so beautiful to experience.

But, we have a problem: Nothing is as misconstrued as love is today. Today, love is more of a transaction. If someone says something nice to you, you love him. Tomorrow if the same person falls short of it, you don't love him that much, or you may even hate him. Even your lifelong friend will seem not so close if he or she says something that offends you or you do not agree with. Why? Where did your love go?

For many people, love is a roll of the dice - a game of chance in which love and hate surface alternately and interchangeably.

And this love-hate relationship is not love at all. It is simply your reaction to a person or a situation - it's subjective. Real love knows no object. It simply exists whether there is an object or not. Real love - unconditional love - is the subject itself. Just like a river flows naturally and people enjoy it at the different places they encounter it, unconditional love exudes from a person, and the people around him will be able to feel it.

In order to discover the quality of your being, that is, love, two things can be done.

First: Repeatedly listen to words of unconditional love so they create a conviction in you - so a space is created in you for the process of transformation.

Second: Meditate so that the transformation can actually happen. In practical life, when you go deeper and deeper into relationships, you will understand all that you feel is not real love but a form of give and take. It is adjustment, compromise, some duty-bound feelings, some fear, some guilt. It is all there in the name of love.

Meditation will take you beyond all the misunderstandings of love because it works at the "being" level. With meditation, a space opens inside you to experience these things clearly for yourself, whatever your age may be.

Understand that when you are able to love without a reason, you will expand. Your world will suddenly seem larger than life. It will be ecstatic! You will become an energy source to yourself and to others. You will be so overflowing that the energy in you has to touch others. There is no other way. Others will be naturally drawn to you.

Real love is the expression of the existential energy in you, and this love can never think of any such arguments. It only knows to flow causelessly. It doesn't know to maintain any track record. The moment you cite incidents from the past, it means that expectations were always there hidden behind your love and, when it is this way, it can never be real love.

Step back and ponder the relationship between a mother and her child. The child loves the mother, expecting her to look after him or her, expecting her to get up at five and pack lunch, expecting her to maintain the child's clothes, without missing a single day. The child adores the mother because he or she enjoys the care, the luxury.

Mothers want to sacrifice for their children, but the attitude with which they sacrifice is what we are talking about. They should do it simply out of an overflowing in them, not out of any hidden expectations. Events will never get recorded in them if they do it out of an overflowing. And even if they get recorded, they will not surface with a vengeance when things happen.

All love that comes with conditions thrives on expectation. No one can deny this, although we may try. The expectation in love is so well woven into it that it is difficult to perceive. That is the problem. Actually, as long as things go smoothly, it is difficult to believe what I am saying. But we hear of so many cases where sons and daughters are written off from the family for simple reasons! Simply because they married outside the community or because there was some feud in the family. Where did all the love go?

Until such incidents, the son or daughter would have been loved very much. What happened? How can it suddenly disappear if it was unconditional love? Real love can never be stopped because it is not bound by any cause-effect cycle. Even in subtle family issues, if you look carefully, you will understand how bound your love is. Just try to rearrange a few things in your life, and watch how your own family reacts.

With your children, as long as you provide for them in the name of love, they also enjoy you, in the name of love. As long as you don't rub each other the wrong way, it's all right. If either of you behaves in an unexpected fashion, the mood of the love changes; the flavor changes. Love that is always under threat is not real love. It is just arranged love. And anything arranged cannot be total. And, when something is not total, it is always under threat. Love needs to be a total celebration, not a duty.

When you can love without a reason, when you can love anything and anyone that comes your way, you will release tremendous energy and beauty. You will appear beautiful irrespective of whether you are physically beautiful or not. Don't think that unconditional love will not get you back anything. It will! But you should evolve to an extent where you see these things coming to you and continue loving, for the sake of loving. Your intelligence will make you see the things that you get in return, and the same intelligence will keep you blissfully untouched by them, also!

There will be a revolutionary change in your heart, and you will be a new person. Others will see a beautiful change in you. They will develop a new respect for you. They will see that you are flowering in a way incomprehensible to them.

To be able to love unconditionally, you need to feel free. What do I mean by free? Not being bound by caste, creed, sect, religion, family, relatives, or any such thing. Because when you are bound by all this, your love will remain bound, and bound love is not real love. How can you love with boundaries? It is against the very definition of love! I am not saying that you should forget your family, religion, etc. Just don't see love in the *context* of all this. Free your inner space from these bondages. When you feel that you belong to the whole of Existence, you can love without any boundaries. And when you take your conditionings away from love, love becomes enlightenment.

Thoughts from Caroline

Trust. Perhaps we trust that we will be able to arrive at work that day, or that the market will have a loaf of bread we can purchase – but how deeply do we trust? Do we believe God is always there for us? Do we believe we will be provided for in a time of need? Do we believe we are always loved? And always loveable? Allowing in the mighty belief that we are always okay, in every moment, and that all is as it should be brings us an immeasurable peace and allows us the freedom to fully embrace each experience that comes into our lives.

Affirmation

"I am loveable, as I am."

Deva Premal

inspirational musician known for her meditative, spiritual songs and chants

I haven't stepped over some invisible boundary from love to unconditional love - it is an ongoing process. I am exploring unconditional love day by day, as we all are. There are moments when I am flooded with a love that feels unconditional, for example, when I am in nature, by the sounds and by the beauty that surround me. I realize there is no need to struggle to become other than I am. I understand in the moment that, like nature, I am unconditionally loved and loving.

I can accept that things are as they are in that moment. This is what I understand to be unconditional, the acceptance of what *is*. How we come to those experiences can be a small moment in the day, such as my moments in nature, or it can be a spiritual journey, or quest, that we partake over a long period of time, such as my journey to learn to love myself unconditionally.

An important part of learning unconditional love is showing it toward oneself because, for some of us, that seems to be the most difficult. For years, I put so many conditions upon myself. I felt that I must do something, that I must accomplish this or that, to become worthy of love. I used to question, if I didn't do those things, was I worthy of love? Was I worthy of loving myself? Now, adjusting my perception to understand that I am loveable exactly as I am - at all times - has been challenging, yet, ultimately, the most rewarding process of my life.

The music I make on this journey has been the mirror of that process, and that process has not always been comfortable! Music is a strong teacher, a very challenging teacher - you could go so far as to call music a living Guru - and it taught me, as did my spiritual teacher Osho, to accept myself the way I am. When I relaxed into "singing my own song," which, in my case, meant sharing the mantras I had grown up with, I felt more and more love toward myself. The Gayatri

Mantra, in particular, holds a special meaning, as my father chanted it for me as a child. I was taught to chant the Gayatri all through my childhood as a goodnight song so it feels not only very auspicious, but, also, an incredible blessing that I am able to share this mantra with so many in the world.

In today's world, we often put "doing" and "being loveable" together, but it is *being* that creates love. What we "do" will never be enough; we won't gain anything by doing things to be loveable. But when we "are" loveable - that is it! Accepting our imperfections, honoring our gifts – I mean, who's perfect, anyway?

An important teacher for me in learning unconditional love is Miten, my partner in life and music. I am so blessed that I can be around him as much as I am and that he is in my life. When we met at Osho's ashram 20 years ago, our hearts instantly connected. And, although we have been together practically 24/7 for those 20 years - mostly spent making music – the love and connection we share continues to deepen and blossom like a flower - unconditionally! I am grateful to have his partnership on my journey.

I have also grown in my understanding of unconditional love by meeting people at our concerts around the world. This grants me the precious gift of seeing the divine in everyone. The concerts Miten, Manose, and I share are invitations for us all - me included - to go beyond the personality, beyond the physical façade and into the Light. And when we meet each other in this unconditional space, it is totally nourishing for the soul. It feels as if we are one, whole, loving entity. We recognize each other as the divine god or goddess that we are - and the music, the chanting, creates that environment.

When we sing the mantras and sacred songs, we are giving and receiving grace. Gratitude and unconditional love are one and the same - because gratitude means that everything that is - right now - is perfect, and there is nothing else to ask for or to pray for. All is as it should be. Yes, it's a mysterious perception and, as I said, certainly a challenging path, but, as Miten sings, "… this is the mountain we all have to climb …" Hari OM!

Out of this, we can do some good in the world. We can participate and contribute. For Miten and I, to immerse ourselves totally into these mantric vibrations means we have become infused with a deep gratitude for what is, and, through this, we can go out and play our part in inspiring peace in the world.

And, that is truly, beyond words, beyond mind - it is where true healing begins.

Thoughts from Caroline

Imagine for a moment that every person on the planet followed his or her passion. That every one of us woke up thankful to participate in the day's activities. Imagine the inspiration and sheer joy humanity would experience. Imagine not simply "making it through the day," but, rather, using divine sparks of inspiration to improve our existence. Imagine rejoicing at the infinite opportunities we have. Imagine grasping that our life is a matter of our own creating. We can imagine all this – and we can become it.

Affirmation

I value my passion and trust my feelings.

Claudio Reilsono

head baseball coach at Carnegie Mellon University, director of pro scouting /
lead scout for the Paramount Scouting Bureau, and motivational speaker

It was August 19,1973, and I was going to my first Pittsburgh Pirates game. My uncle worked at Three Rivers Stadium in a place called "The Allegheny Club," a country club-like restaurant inside the stadium. My Italian-born parents were not baseball fans. Neither was I. But, I was bored that summer and going to the game gave me something to do.

As we got closer to Pittsburgh, I laid eyes on a round, cement building. I had never seen anything like it before. It was Three Rivers Stadium, and it was huge! As we got closer, my amazement only grew.

Inside, we took the elevator to the club floor. When the door opened, I smelled something vague but unique in the air. Pictures of baseball and football players lined the walls. I had no idea who any of the players were, except for one: the late Roberto Clemente, who had passed away eight months earlier.

As I walked down the hallway, I could see a seemingly endless, green baseball field surrounded by red and yellow seats. We had arrived early, before anyone was in the stands, and the emptiness made the Stadium look bigger than it was. I was amazed at the size of it. Then, with visions of the field still in my head, I followed my uncle into the locker room. I couldn't believe it! There, laughing and playing around in their sparkling white uniforms, were the Pirates!

Finally, intent on giving me the full tour, my uncle took me onto the field through the dugout. Wow! My jaw dropped. I felt so small! I had never felt like that before. I was totally speechless. The game hadn't even started, and I was mesmerized. Then, the first pitch was thrown, and that was it. I was in love!

When I got home, my Mom, Ida, and my Dad, Olindo, asked me if I had a good time.

"I did," I said, "And, I think I know what I want to do for the rest of my life! I want to be in professional baseball!"

Instead of saying, "Yeah, ok, son," patting me on the head and pushing me away, my dad did what few parents would do. He put his hand on my shoulder and said, "If that's what you want to do, I will make sure I do all I can do to give you the opportunity to make your dreams come true. I love you."

My mom said, "As long as you don't get hurt and you do well in school, I will do whatever I can for you. I love you."

Despite my aspirations, I was no different from the other kids my age; every kid in Pittsburgh said he wanted to be a baseball player when he grew up. But, I stuck with it, and my parents stuck with it. That made all the difference. While the other kids' parents never took them seriously, my parents made my dream a focal point in our lives. They provided me with all the support I could ever need.

And, it was a good thing they did. Throughout the years, the rest of my family members were as quick with their criticisms as my parents were with their praise. At every family get-together I was told to grow up, to be realistic, and, "You'll never make it … It's a pipe dream!"

I was hurt. These were people I truly cared about. But, my parents fought for me. They told the rest of our family members to mind their own business, and they were quick to reassure me. "Whatever it takes, however long it takes, you are going to get there!" they said. "Just keep at it."

Tryouts came and went. I was injured during one. I bombed another. Finally, at age 22, I decided I was done as a player. I decided coaching would perhaps be a better route for me. In February of 1988, I was named head coach at my old high school, Quaker Valley. I was 23, and the youngest head coach in the league. I was ecstatic! I loved coaching. I had great players. My parents loved watching me. I felt I was on my way.

Just a few months later, on May 18, we found out my mother had cancer. She was my best friend. When she passed away on October 8, 1988, I was crushed. She was only 48.

At the funeral, I was devastated. I leaned down to kiss her, and it was the first time she didn't kiss back. I was beside myself with grief. I could think of nothing but her, that she was gone. I felt my life had changed forever, and that perhaps my relatives were right. Maybe it was time to give up baseball, grow up, and learn to be a man.

But, then, my dad came over, put his hand on my shoulder, and said, "Claud, I know what you are thinking, and you can't give up. You are the only thing that can keep her dream alive." That sealed it! I decided nothing was going to stop me from realizing my dream! Nothing and no one!

As the years went by, I coached at a number of different schools. When I was 25, I was the head coach at Penn State (Beaver Satellite Campus.) On October 8, 1990, we won the championship! It was my dad's birthday and the two-year anniversary of my mom's passing. I felt then that my baseball dreams would finally be realized. It seemed I was destined to make it.

But, I still had not reached my goal. I wanted to be in the pros! After over 140 rejection letters, I finally got a chance in 2001, at the age of 36. A man named James L. Gamble gave me my first pro job as a professional baseball scout! I did it! We did it! My mother would have been so proud.

Today, I am the head baseball coach at Carnegie Mellon University and the director of pro scouting/lead scout for the Paramount Scouting Bureau. I have signed over 60 players to pro contracts all over the world, and I'm one of the top scouts in professional baseball. I talk on radio and television shows, am an ESPN radio guest, and have actually hired major league players I was a fan of to work for my company. I announce boxing matches and have been asked to play in "celebrity" golf tournaments. I have speaking engagements, write for sports magazines, and have been hired to do instructional camps. I've even acted in a movie.

I attribute all of my success to my parents. Their love for me - their belief in me - gave me the opportunity to go after my dreams, no matter how tough it got. It didn't matter that other people my age were on their way in life when I felt stuck in place. It didn't matter what people said. My parents pushed me, they supported me, and their love made me push toward my dreams that much more. When I was down, they picked me up. When I was rejected, they told me I was getting closer to a "yes." They lived for me. I lived for them. They were always there to motivate me. They were my biggest fans.

There is an old saying, "If you ever see a turtle on top of a fence post, you know he didn't get there alone." I certainly didn't get here alone. My parents were instrumental in everything I've achieved. I am thankful that my dad, who passed in 2004, was able to see it all happen.

Now, I have a wonderful wife, Lynda, and a wonderful daughter, Ida, who we named after my mom. One day, nine-year-old Ida went to the library for a writing and drawing program. When she came home that afternoon, I asked her if she liked the program.

She answered, "I did, Daddy. I want to be an author and an illustrator."

I grinned. "I will do whatever I can to give you the opportunity to make your dream come true. I love you."

Thoughts from Caroline

Inside all of us, there is a yearning. A yearning to be understood and accepted and loved on all levels. We will reach a day when this unconditional love is given and received by everyone. For now, we are able to learn it through divine relationships. A precious gift, these relationships can help us evolve rapidly and in ways beyond what we are able to do on our own. What a blessing when we choose to be open to them!

Affirmation

I embrace spiritual relationships as opportunities

to grow exponentially in love.

Love Like God

Dea Shandera

highly-regarded entertainment and media executive / consultant working on projects that enlighten and celebrate the human spirit

Brent N. Hunter

author of "The Rainbow Bridge" and a seasoned information technology executive

---

They were navigating through their richly rewarding, full, busy, Spirit-filled lives when it happened. She hadn't been romantically involved with anyone for seven years, and he hadn't been involved for several years, either. They weren't even looking for love. They had decided that without that more-than-special, deep connection with another person it would be preferable to be alone.

In a divine orchestration, Brent and Dea were introduced as a few hundred people gathered to celebrate the life of Francis X. Maguire (Frank,) a businessman, public speaker, author of "You're the Greatest," and a one-of-a-kind gorgeous soul whose life's work was about deeply validating people. It seems Frank had been busy with a host of other angels to ensure the moment came together in perfect harmony with the universe. It was as though the billions of moments Brent and Dea had lived prepared them for their experience of meeting. It was clear the timing was right. Perhaps months or years before, they may not have even recognized each other's souls.

Brent had been meditating since he was twelve years old, a gift from his father, and his senses were keen, as Spirit would illuminate connections for him - be they personal or professional. He later revealed to Dea that he knew of their deep connection after only three seconds of looking into her eyes and hearing her voice.

Dea felt something, too, but she was also feeling shy, not fully recognizing the depth of the connection. Like a flower gently opening, there was something magical and mystical taking place within her – and it was undeniable.

As part of their early exploration, Brent wanted to give Dea a copy of the second edition of "The Rainbow Bridge," one of the books he had written. Dea was busy with her own entertainment and media consulting business and let Brent know that, although she was excited to read his work, he would have to be patient, as it may take her a while to find the time.

Spirit had other plans. When the book arrived by mail, Dea was inspired to read it immediately and postponed all of her work that day. She discovered that the words soared into her heart and soul, as deep recognition began to flood her being. She felt that the words Brent had written in his book had actually come from within her. Her soul blossomed to see the kindred spirit with whom she had spent many love-filled lifetimes and whose mission in this life, to make the world a better place in so many ways, matched hers as if they were twins. It didn't take Dea long to begin to understand what was happening. Life was suddenly new and amazing, in ways beyond her wildest dreams!

Dea and Brent lived a few hundred miles away from each other so they began to communicate by phone. During the first of many calls, Brent shared that he would love to visit for a weekend to get to know Dea better. Much to her own surprise, Dea found herself offering Brent the opportunity to stay at her home on his first visit. While this was out of character for her, somehow she felt it was impossible to think of him as a stranger or as someone she had just met.

Marked by a full moon eclipse, they both felt eager anticipation for their first weekend together, and, during that visit, they began with a deeply spiritual ceremony. Each spoke of their desire for a better world for all – filled with love, peace, harmony, freedom, and all needs met for every member of the human family. Blessings were also sent out for Mother Earth in all her beauty. Their connection, begun in such a spiritual and purposeful manner, was deep, comfortable, and familiar. Yet, it was still filled with mystery about what it might become.

Brent introduced Dea to a beautiful Mayan phrase during their first weekend, "In La 'Kesh," which means, "I am another you" or "You and I are one." This resonated with both of them, as each conversation and time together revealed two souls who were most likely twin flames, where mystical and unconditional love described their blessed union.

Unconditional love serves as the foundation for the mystical love relationship between Brent and Dea. There is almost no ego, there is a constant merging, a unity, a union filled with wonder, excitement, innocence, humor, and a deep caring and interest in everything inside the mind, heart, and soul of one another. A respect for their differences and a constant celebration of their synergy ... breathtaking in its scope and splendor.

The thoughtfulness that happens between them and the flow of gifts beginning with time spent together is beautiful to witness. The unconditional basis for their love is organic and comes with a deep sense of responsibility to stay in the flow, where neither comes to the blessed union with expectations or demands, but continues to show up even when what's happening takes all the patience and flexibility of a lifelong yogi.

The day-to-day unconditional love in this new and expanding relationship inspired many new dreams, including the desire to partner and work together on many projects that were near and dear to each of them. They found that co-creating was fun and easy with a flow that had divine fingerprints on it, and the more they experienced this, the more they wanted to collaborate with one another.

Gratitude plays an important role in this unconditional, mystical love connection. Everything that Brent and Dea put forth into the relationship is recognized and appreciated with intention by each in a way that is natural, open, verbal, and affectionate.

Many times words cannot fully express feelings. Brent and Dea recognize each other as "beloved," "gifts from God," and as their own "dream come true." They are flowing with these sentiments with one another, and the joy and bliss they feel constantly grows every time they connect.

Humor is another important element of their deep connection. From the beginning, they giggled with the innocence of children. Fun and laughter coupled with joy and bliss give them cause to celebrate everything!

Early on, Brent and Dea made a conscious decision to meet every night during their dreams. Neither had thought to do this at any other point, with anyone else in their lives, but it seemed natural between them. This ritual gave them a comfort level that transcends the time they spend together. Even on those nights when they are blessed to fall asleep in one another's arms, they meet in their dreams.

When unconditional love is nurtured and growing - it can often show from the inside out. Dea has been stopped by strangers who claim she is glowing, and people who connect with her over the phone notice it, too. When Brent and Dea are in public, people have remarked they wish they could bottle and sell the magical energy between them. There is something about going with the flow of the river of love and not trying to direct it that makes the journey so much sweeter.

On one visit, Brent wanted to go over every word and picture that made up the two large vision boards Dea had created a few years before. His beautiful intention, which touched Dea at the depths of her soul, was to help her anchor her dreams and desires. She hadn't spent much time looking at the boards since she made them, but they had proven effective anyway.

As they stood together, with their arms around each other, studying each board, they realized nearly every word and visual prayer had been answered, and most of them connected into Brent. Special words that held great meaning for them as a couple were clearly glued in prominent places and were now anchored into reality. It was a magical moment.

Brent and Dea practice taking an active role in anchoring each other's prayers and dreams, and the powerful nature of two united in vision and intention is nothing short of astonishing.

Brent and Dea recognize that their mystical and unconditional love for each other not only affects them, but it affects everyone around them. It spreads with a positive ripple to people all over the world. It is always a joy to share their love, and they get excited to know it is contagious for those who witness their bliss. Many have mentioned how they become filled with faith and hope that this can happen for them as well.

One of the things we've learned in this relationship is how to deal with the other's needs and desires - riding the fine line between that concept and expectations. It has become clear that if either of us comes from a place of male or female psyche, we have a separation from each other, and it can cause a little bump in the road until one of us lovingly brings it to the other's attention.

If we initiate words or actions coming from a place of ego, it would also be highlighted to both of us with a gentle knowing that we had veered from the center of the road, which is where we like to be because it's a comfortable and healthy place of love, compassion, and compromise.

We highly recommend communication when something arises that might push an old button. We strive for being button-less, but, being human, we are still in that process.

Although a deep love was present from the beginning, we allowed other aspects of the relationship to unfold in their own divine timing. By meeting during dreamtime – consciously or subconsciously – we felt as though we consummated the relationship in the dreamtime before the three-dimensional experience. Playing and giggling together in that realm brought us closer quickly. Both of us remembered bits and pieces of what happened during the intentional dreamtime connection, but mostly it was a feeling of remembering our familiarity from past lives. Every last communication of any given day has included that we will see each other in our dreams.

We also aspire to follow an approach of non-attachment and equanimity because when one of us wants something that the other prefers not to go toward in that moment, it is more organic and effortless to have little - and hopefully no - attachment to the outcome.

Even the most mystical and unconditional love-filled relationship needs patience, nurturing, and is always growing, but we know it's worth it. In fact, one of the reasons we have come together in this relationship is to work on our life lessons and grow through our experiences together. How wonderful it is to grow in a safe and unconditionally loving environment!

Another aspect of unconditional love for us is our responsibility to practice staying in the present moment while loving each other through the growth and changes that happen over time. We recognize these changes may not match our heart's desire and could lead to some of our greatest challenges. If we make it our intention to begin discovering the perfection of what is and begin embracing the mystery and the unfolding of our relationship – dropping our need to know all the answers - the sweetest unconditional love can be ours. Through the power of love, those barriers can be broken, and the view on the other side of that bridge is definitely worth the journey!

Thoughts from Caroline

What blame are we holding that keeps us from moving forward? When we understand that acceptance and contentment are within us at all times, it allows us to re-frame the experiences we feel have caused us harm. What are we able to learn from the situation or from the person? What value can be found? And, what are we holding against someone, in this moment, that we can release?

Affirmation

" I release judgments of myself and others, trusting we are all on our best path. "

Lorelei Shellist

keynote speaker, life coach and counselor, and author of "Runway Run Away: A Backstage Pass to Fashion, Romance & Rock 'n Roll"

Buddie taught me everything I needed to learn about unconditional love. She was a dog. A good dog. A loyal dog. An independent dog with a life of her own, friends of her own, and a path of her own. Sometimes it seemed she loved others more than she loved me, but she always stayed by me. I had to learn to let her love others without judging her for it or taking it personally. I had to trust that she loved me, no matter what. That is why, I believe, dog is God spelled backwards.

Unconditional love. It doesn't state, "I will love you, *if*...." It says, "I love you no matter what." No matter if you aren't perfect. No matter if you snore. No matter if you work too hard and come home grumpy, bitchy, or tired. I still love you. But, what if you do something I consider bad or hurtful to me? Is that possible, that you could do something *to* me? Or is that just the way I see it - so I can turn around and blame you, and I won't have to take responsibility for what I am experiencing with you?

In my life, there have been so many conditions ... just to get a job, just to get through school, just to get along. The world taught me that I would be more accepted, or more loved, if I would just do this or that. As a result, I got pretty good at becoming a people pleaser: pleasing others so that I would be more loved. I also believed that if I tried to get others to please me, then I would love them. Boy, did I have it wrong ... or at least *misunderstood.* I was on a merry-go-round. Eventually I learned that my people pleasing only served to keep others at a distance.

Loving with conditions keeps us under the false belief that we are in control. I have clearly been a perpetrator of this. When I was younger, I fell deeply in love with a sweet, shy, sensitive guy. He was my knight in shining armor, except when he drank. If I could only control his drinking, everything would be okay. I used love as a weapon, instead of a *quality*. Imagine: Love as a quality. I had no understanding of this. What I thought was, if I controlled my level of loving, I could get him to do what I wanted him to do - such as stop drinking.

"Maynard," I would say, "I simply cannot marry you until you stop drinking!" That was my condition. If he would behave the way I wanted him to behave, then I would give myself to him unconditionally.

Needless to say, it didn't work. My poor, darling fiancé died at the age of thirty, trying to self-medicate in order to fight his own demons and diseases. I ended up without a husband and without children. A steep price to pay for loving under those conditions and under the *mis*belief that I could control anything. If I'd known then what I know now, would I have loved him differently? YES.

Unconditional love starts with the self. When I am in love with my-Self, there is no reason to find fault with others. I have no judgment on anything, and therefore love may exist without conditions. It is when I get caught up in what's right, wrong, good, bad, or ugly that I get into trouble and nothing goes my way. Who am I to judge anything as anything other than *love*? Pure and simple - but easier said than done. Like medicine, yoga, music, and sports, to love unconditionally takes practice.

Unconditional love continues with *acceptance*. Acceptance of "what is." Perfect in God's world, our world, and this world - if we could just see it that way. Things are the way they are, for reasons we don't know ... yet.

What does this mean, the acceptance of *what is*? It means taking the judgment out of the circumstance. Not judging anything as wrong, bad, or even untimely. When someone dies at a young age we say, "Oh, he or she died an *untimely* death." What does that mean? How do we really know what time someone should have died?

The truth is he or she died right when they were supposed to die. Not too early, not too late. So our only choice is to accept this death for when it is and what it is and continue to pour on the love. Especially for ourselves, because in those times when someone close to us dies, it is *our* loss we grieve ... not his or hers. So we begin to accept and love ourselves through those challenging times - without judging our processes or God's timing. Instead, we learn to *accept*.

Unconditional love does not *judge*. My professor, Dr. Ron Hulnick at the University of Santa Monica, always says, "God is not in the business of judging, so why should I be?" He reminds his students that we don't always know the deeper reasons why certain things happen to people. Perhaps there is a spiritual history going back through many lifetimes that has brought this person, or this group of people, to this place and time where their human experience has been chosen for their highest good. We have no way of knowing what their highest good is. Therefore, we have no basis on which to judge them.

As the saying goes, "There are three sides to the truth: yours, mine, and God's." Who are we to judge? Judging others and judging ourselves is the opposite of unconditional love. How can we possibly be loving if we are busy judging?

Still, it is part of the evolution of the soul to become aware of our judgments in order to clear and release them once and for all. How do we do that? Ah ...we learn to forgive.

Unconditional love is *forgiveness*. I've heard it said that to forgive is to "give as you gave before." Sort of like wiping the slate clean. Once we begin to acknowledge our judgments of others - and ourselves - we can dig deeper and discover what irrational beliefs we are holding. These *mis*beliefs or *mis*understandings may have come from our childhoods, our parents, or other authority figures. We may have inherited them, or we may have deduced them from a situation or circumstance that we were not even aware of at the time. For example ...

I was living in New York City and had a group of friends who played softball every week in Central Park. I used to go, hoping I'd get to play. When I was in grade school, I never got picked for team sports, or, if I did, I'd sit on the bench. Still, I figured, I'd give it a try.

As it turned out, I was pretty darn good at the game! I had quick instincts and long legs, and I ran fast. Soon the team captains recognized my agility and would pick me to play second base. As time went on, I realized I could have been a lot better at this sport, "if only..." If only I had brothers, if only my father had spent more time with me and played sports with me or encouraged my athletic abilities. But, I didn't have any brothers, and the attention I got was for my looks and girlish graces. Be pretty, become a model, and find a husband! That is what my parents wanted for me, or so I believed.

As the summer softball games in Central Park continued, I became much more a part of the team, and I got better and better. I began to discover that I was good at other sports, too, but I felt like I was never quite *good enough*. I never won any awards, and I was already in my thirties so there was nowhere to go with my sports dreams. Who was to blame? There must be someone I could blame! Surely it wasn't *my* fault that I wasn't nurtured or coached in sports. It wasn't my mother's fault for not giving me a brother. It had to be my father!

And so, my story began: "If only my father would have played sports with me, I could have had a serious career in sports!" That became my opinion and my judgment. I was upset with my father because he wasn't "fatherly" enough. He didn't pay enough attention to my needs or to what I wanted; in fact, his fathering was just *not good enough*.

Fast-forward 15 years to when I became aware of my judgments and misbeliefs and learned forgiveness. My father was approaching his 90th birthday, and my mother had already passed on. I was finally at a stage in life where I wanted to unravel my stories - these stories and misunderstandings I had been carrying unknowingly for so long. In the last year of my father's life, I began to talk to him and share my thoughts about these things.

One day I said, "You know, Dad, I'm a pretty good athlete. I wish
you had spent more time with me, playing ball and stuff when I was
a kid. I could've excelled in sports!"

My father's reply? "Aw, bullshit, you wanted to go to the beach! I
used to drive you to the beach and pick you up; that's all you wanted
to do! I was just letting you do what you wanted to do."

I was stunned. He was right. I loved the beach. To this day, they
call me the Mermaid, and body surfing is my favorite sport. I love
dolphins and whales and sand between my toes.

All this time I had been judging my father for some story, some
misbelief I had bought into. I had judged him as not good enough,
but, even worse, when I went inside, underneath it all, I was judging
myself as not good enough. I was self-loathing without even realizing
it.

As I worked with this new awareness, I discovered I was judging
myself as "not good enough" in so many ways ... and so I could
never win. I could never be at peace and accept things as they were.
I had to learn how to *forgive*. Forgive my father for something he
hadn't done and forgive myself for believing he had done it. I took
full responsibility and began the mantra in service to healing my-
Self: "I forgive my-Self for judging my father as not good enough in
the first place. I forgive my-Self for judging my-Self as less than, as
ignored, as neglected, and as ... not good enough."

The dam broke. I cried and cried until every tear had shed itself from
the well of judgments deep inside my soul. All those years I had held
those irrational beliefs that I wasn't good enough, that nothing was
good enough, and that no one would ever be good enough. Judging,
judging, judging. Those tears of forgiveness opened the gates to a
new awareness that all those things I thought were just misbeliefs. I
forgave my-Self for having those thoughts at all. In my forgiveness, I
was able to wipe everything clean. From that perspective, I could see
that this was an opportunity for me to heal, to grow, to accept my-
Self as I am - as good enough and, even better, as perfect in God's
eyes!

I am so grateful I was able to share this with my father before he died. It opened my eyes to the many grudges I held against my parents. I began to heal them all, one at a time, and to learn to love them and myself unconditionally. The more I practice this, the more I learn to love the world without judgment. I remember what Jesus said on the cross, "Father forgive them, for they know not what they do." Sometimes we just don't know any better. I was able to love my father again in a new way and to love my-Self unconditionally. To love my-Self, no matter what, and to be *grateful* for the lessons I have learned, even through my misinterpretations of the truth.

Unconditional love means being grateful. (Otherwise said, "full of greatness.") Knowing and trusting that all things are good, no matter what. Being and staying in the loving energy even when times are adverse. Looking for the lessons in life experiences, like sifting through gravel and finding the gold. Loving under any condition and being grateful for those people, places, and things that are here to teach us about ourselves. Loving our-Selves under any and every condition there may be. Loving our-Selves through the toughest times, especially when we are challenged, scared, angry, or sad. Loving ourselves, and others, through it all. Loving simply for the sake of loving, just like Buddie loved.

ghts from Caroline

In a world full of love, it is up to us to choose to recognize that love. We can enlarge our scope of vision beyond our pursuits and goals and perceived complications to allow love to enter. When we wonder, "What is the point of our existence?" the answer always comes down to love. We are rewarded with a richer, fuller existence when we remember love and when we embrace it in all its forms.

In the middle of this book, in a thoughtful

Affirmation

I choose to allow love into my life.

Love Like God

Dr. Joseph Shrand

instructor of psychiatry at Harvard Medical School, medical director of CASTLE, and assistant child psychiatrist on the medical staff of Massachusetts General Hospital

In the summer of 1978, I was working as the camp counselor of a cabin load of seven-year-olds who had been sent to overnight camp in upstate New York. The counselors had arrived a few days before the campers to "team build," and I found myself sitting in a large recreation room, one of many strangers in a circle of strangers. There seemed no interesting prospects for a summer romance, and I resigned myself to a long and uninspiring summer.

And, then it happened. Across the room entered a new camp counselor, backlit by the sun. She was beautiful. Long hair the color of a warm russet topped gently by a black beret, a rainbow shirt with the promise of hidden treasure, jeans, and multicolored sandals. She sat in a metal-back chair, as did I, but far away across the room. I was riveted, as was every other male counselor there. Summer became more interesting instantly!

The group leader ended an exercise and asked us to break into smaller groups for the next one. I wondered how I was going to get across the room to sit next to her. And then, to my astonishment, she fixed her gaze, walked across the room, and asked me if she could sit in the empty steel-back metal chair next to mine.

This was my moment to be cool. So I looked up at her and said, "Bluhbbbllmummmnph!"

She sat down anyway.

And that is how I met Carol. Both of us were 19 years old. Both of us were far from home, but our homes were remarkably only 45 minutes apart. Imagine. Here we were, a six-hour drive from home, with other campers from all over New England and New York State, and we lived less than an hour away from each other.

Perhaps those who have never experienced love-at-first-sight consider it a myth. But, for me, it was real and true, and, right away, we felt like we had known each other in a previous lifetime. Within days, other counselors wondered if we had known each other before, and we wondered the same. One of the other group leaders commented that I hadn't even given the other guys a chance. It was a done deal from the moment Carol and I met. I had fallen in love without condition.

At least until the end of the camp. And, until the end of our first year together in Boston. And, again, almost to the end of college, a long-distance romance, and a sad but honest awareness that we were still too young to make a lifelong commitment. That we should be open to other possibilities, date other people, and not have any "what if's" in our lives.

We decided we were still too young, at 22, to make a conscious decision about marriage and a commitment to embrace that unconditional love. But, within the passion of our courtship, there were unconditional moments, glimmers of a future. There were also times harshly evaluative, critical, uncertain, pushing the other to wonder about who we were as people and as a couple, and learning to integrate without losing the individuality of who we were. Unconditional love did not mean total satisfaction and certainly did not mean complacency.

Eight years after meeting, we shared the promise of unconditional love and became engaged. We left behind our families and drove off in a white, two-door Mazda with no air conditioning, pulling along our U-Haul full of expectations, and singing, "We're living in sin, in sin, in sin, in sin, in Cincinnati!" We knew no one in Ohio. But, I was going to the University of Cincinnati Medical School to become a doctor, and Carol began work as a university photographer.

On the first day of classes, I walked into the auditorium that would be my home for the next two years, before I ventured into hospitals and touched real people. Getting in had been very competitive, which meant I was in the room with over 100 young men and women who had to be equally, if not more, qualified to be in this amphitheater. Perhaps recognizing her audience, our training director had drawn in stark, white chalk on the pristine blackboard of the Class of 1990 this intriguing equation:

$$P = MD$$

She was trying to tell us to relax. All you had to do was pass your classes, and you would be awarded an MD degree. You would graduate medical school.

I don't think anyone felt a micron more at ease.

Medical school was as hard and grueling as advertised. Hours of lectures bookended by hours of studying. $P = MD$, although probably true, was not an equation many students followed. Grades far above a "P" were personal expectations and seemed to carry the weight of a future residency placement from the very first exam. Competitive as it was to get into medical school, getting a top residency after graduation was even more so, as the number of spots were so much fewer. And, residency was the step toward fellowship, which was the step to a medical career that mattered. The hell with $P = MD$. Get the A!

I met an instructor, a big, burly physician, who believed in "The Monastic Life of Medicine." To him, medicine was everything. His days and nights revolved around his beeper, his availability to his patients, and to his research. He cajoled and seduced us to do the same. We were medical students now, and medicine should be our lives.

My dad believed the same. My father's love for medicine was all-encompassing. His work as a pediatrician was his identity; his commitment to his patients was a fact of life. Sometimes, when I was a child, I would have to wait for hours for him to pick me up from school, and I often tolerated the disappointment of having him cancel our scheduled time together.

Dad's patients came first. They loved him, and he loved being loved by them. He was masterful, soothing, trustworthy, and always available. I would sit with him in his office, and watch in wonder as he looked into the ears of his tiny ward or playfully put a child at ease while giving an inoculation. There, in his office, he was my hero. He taught me that the love of medicine was a harsh mistress and required a complete surrender to the professional. Anything could and must be sacrificed for medicine: marriage, family, sleep, money, and time.

So I studied. And studied. I kept studying, a room in our small apartment devoted entirely to my medical books, sitting at the desk my dad had given me where I would absorb the knowledge I needed to "Do No Harm." The first exam was in Anatomy on the muscles of the back. I studied and studied. Trapezius. Latissimus Dorsi, Levator Scapulie. Where they were. To what they attached. What they moved.

Carol would come into the study and beam a smile that previously would effortlessly entice me to go out for dinner. But, her smile had first to overcome the barrier of a wall plastered with anatomy posters, a hurricane of worksheets, and a mountain made of text books. And medical soldier that I was, I would say, "No, I have to study. I am in medical school. This is the most important thing in my life." Her smile diminished, she would close the door.

And, I would study.

I took my first exam in medical school and failed it cold. Dejected and despondent, I walked home to the apartment. I lost my medical school ID on the way, which I interpreted as an unconscious acknowledgement that I was not meant to be a doctor.

When I got home, Carol was there. She looked at me, recognized I was defeated, and gave me a hug. In that moment, my entire life changed. My priorities became clear.

No matter how hard I worked, medical school or medicine would never give me a hug. But, Carol would. Carol would *always* give me a hug. And, even as I strove to be a doctor, I was in jeopardy of doing *great* harm, abandoning a love from which I had grown for almost a decade.

I tell this story to every medical student, resident, nurse, social worker, anyone who I have the honor and privilege to teach. And, to anyone who will listen. No matter how hard we work, no matter how much energy and commitment we put into our business, none of that will ever give us a hug. But your partner will, your family will. If you have kids, it is their hugs that matter. Job security? Forget it. Family security? It is up to you. It was up to me. Family first.

Since that immortal hug, Carol has remained supportive of me and my career. She *knows* that if there was a choice to make between work and home, it would be home that would be the choice. As a result of my transformation, I have had the fortune to get the residency I wanted, the fellowship I wanted, to become one of the youngest medical directors of child psychiatry at an internationally known hospital, and to have the honor and privilege of working with amazing people over these last 20 years as a child psychiatrist. I love going to work, and I love coming home. For there, at home, is Carol. With a hug.

Thoughts from Caroline

What communications are we missing? Are we allowing the voices of animals or our angels to reach us? Are we too busy to hear the voice of God? We can benefit from opening our perception to the messages that are all around us. Look into the eyes of a dolphin, and you will recognize each other. Smell the scent of a flower, and you will sense the presence of God. Nature presents us with so many gifts; it is up to us to choose to see them.

Affirmation

I see beauty and love in all life forms.

Leesa Sklover, Ph.D

pioneer in integrative medicine and sound-music healing, composer and performer of sacred and trans-species music, spiritual counselor / educator, cetacean researcher, and shamanic healer

As a little girl, I would often sing the Leslie Bricusse lyrics from the musical Dr Doolittle: "I do not understand the human race. It has so little love for creatures with a different face. Treating animals like people is no madness or disgrace. I do not understand the human race."

The musical's "Rex Harrison" was my inspiration. He made me believe I could talk to and think like animals. The film showed him as he found the giant, pink sea snail with the assistance of the dolphins. I wanted to have them help me, too. It seemed possible to speak to them non-locally, telepathically, from a place of love within a heart-centered reality.

That heart-centered reality exists and is based on Pearsall's energy cardiology, which suggests that the heart is the conductor of communication and hums with the cells of the being with whom we are engaged. Today, as a researcher and advocate for cetaceans in the wild, the living cells in my heart commune with the heartsong and cellular connections of the moving cetaceans.

I have been blessed with the amazing gift to see images and hear the feelings of other moving beings. I am told I am a bridge, which represents inner worlds that may not meet. I was a receptor even as a child. In my twenties, my ability was validated through a telepathy experiment I was in on "Nightline." It proved I could see images, at a distance. My validated ability brought with it new confidence, and I was able to sense the feelings of animals with greater ease.

The cetaceans use sound and touch for expressing themselves socially. Through these senses, they can express tenderness and anger. Housed within their giant brains is a capacity for intelligence and emotion that equals or surpasses our own. The use of ecolocation, communication at a distance, clearly indicates their intuitive ability to trust a much larger world environment than the microcosm in which man involves himself. When I connect with and commune with the cetaceans of the world, I try not to put my humanness on to them. Mirroring what they present is how I honor and love them.

The animals of the Palaeolithic period carried the wisdom and the secrets of life. The wisdom of animal medicine considers them the "secret keepers." I find this is true when I am in their company over a period of days. Together, we experience time on their terms and commune with one another in an altered reality.

In many of the societies where animals are honored and communed with as moving beings, the humans experience major psychological trauma when they have to kill their fellow creatures for food (a subsistence practice separate from the whaling trauma occuring in Japan and Norway.)

Myths were created to help man come to terms with the murder of their soul friends. Dolphin Medicine is what Native Americans and aboriginal-mystical cultures refer to as the qualities of the dolphin that is part human.

Throughout mythology, the trans-species link between man and dolphin has been expressed. The merpeople of Mu, off the Hawaiian islands, were forced to transform into part dolphin in order to save themselves. This dual body has become the mermaid symbol. The Minoans see dolphins as having a direct genealogical link to humans. The Cretans saw the dolphin as God. No wonder we feel a hypnotic, altered state in their presence – we have believed in our connection for millennia!

And, it isn't just a myth - we can communicate with cetaceans. They hear us. My friend, President of Cetacean Society International Bill Rossiter, shared a story with me of the time when a sperm whale called "Physty" responded to the Bach my friend was playing. When Bill asked Physty, "How do you feel? What do you want?" the whale responded by moving to the net that led out to the open ocean. This is just one example of a number of stories.

I wrote a play 25 years ago called, "When Parallels Touch," in which I shared how human relationships from two very different worlds/cultures share common emotional experiences. Human-nonhuman relationships are meant to honor the dolphin from the dolphin's point of view and to represent the whale from the whale's perceptual world. I am aligned with the animals' psychological and emotional comparability. The reality and non-linear reality of my experiences with these beings created in me a life-long love affair that arose the moment I first met one. My imprints of their messages remain in me forever.

One experience, one look can steal your heart. I remember saying, "I am in love" when I saw the beluga I worked with in Canada with a group that protected lone cetaceans. That whale came back to us daily in search of company. He would swim to the side of the boat, tilt his head, and look at us eye to eye. It was the peak of interspecies love! I felt the same ecstatic connection as when I love another human.

That whale still haunts me. Many things came from my heartstrings humming for those days out there with him, in the fog. Looking for him, seeing him follow our boat until he could not keep up, realizing the heart-wrenching reality that I would not be back the next day. He would be out there in the sea alone for a long time, forever, alone in the blue. I felt the heartstrings left behind.

At night, I sometimes dream about him. In my dreams, he is alone in the harbor with only the bell buoy to comfort him. It breaks my heart to have had to leave him. The sound is what he connected to as his mother, as his family. The only way I could manage was to write about my experience in the fictional novella, "Belugaman."

Though I have grown and worked in integrative medicine, psychology, music performance, music business, music therapy, academia, and ecopsychology, my longing to be Dr. Doolittle has never left me. In my opinion, the best way to realize my dream is through music. By becoming a music-therapist/singer I have been given a new language to express my ability intuitively in human healing and in the cetacean world. I call what I do transsinging because out loud or inside my mind, I send a vibroacoustic message in the same way a bioelectromagnetic field is emitted and used in energy healing.

The cetacean is a superior being largely beyond our grasp. I honor that being's inner psychic world, and this sense of honor allows me great insight into the nature of reality. It is what I encourage in my work with humans: the ability to listen in silence to an inner psychic world. I feel that this trans-humanimal bond is best expressed in sound, intuitive reception, and bi-unicommunication.

Once, I was in Hawaii singing to, hearing, and swimming with an approaching pod when it occurred to me that *this* was how they were meant to be experienced. In partnership with Jim Nollman, I made music that honored the cetaceans and sang with them on their terms. I learned that what they present can only be mirrored; I cannot begin the song.

Studies show that depressed individuals who have had contact or seen an image of a dolphin feel better. But, it is not their purpose to make us happy. There must be ways to learn from their essence, without imparting our needs on them. I must listen to the inner music within them and not push my song or agenda on them. I must mirror them where they are.

I am guilty of my past experiences: swimming on the backs of dolphins two at a time in Mexico, holding on to a fin in Florida, touching soft, blubbery skin. As a child, I would pet them in lagoons. Once, I touched a Beluga tongue at an aquarium. While I cannot deny the thrill these experiences gave me, once I could hear them, I realized they held a great sadness. This realization made me feel the need to free them.

Years later, I found myself doing just that, in combination with environmentalists and scientists as research director of the International Cetacean Society. Unconditional love of these free and wild beings means that we must leave them alone and watch from a little further away most of the time.

Although they may be difficult to comprehend, there are endless stories of attempts from both sides to bridge the divide between the cetaceans and us. The San Francisco Chronicle reported a story of men who rescued a drowning humpback trapped in crab traps. They risked themselves to free the whale. Afterward, the whale swam about them in joy, nudged each person in thanks, and watched every move of the man who cut the cord.

My moments of whale love have led me to give back. Perhaps the more we know, the more we can rethink our ethical landscape and love and understand them from their perspective. It is hard to know what they feel. I continue the attempt as a way to give back what they have given me.

The field of trans-species psychology, developed by G.A. Bradshaw, creates the cognitive and emotional model of behavior for all animals, including humans. She links the inner world of humans and animals together in a place of equality. I bow to the whales and dolphins I have known in the wild and in captivity. They are their own divine species with unique thought forms, senses, and feelings. Yet, despite their uniqueness, many of their feelings are the same as ours.

In response to my experience with these beings and the experiences of others, I have conceived the "1 Whale - 1 Child Project" with an educator, a film and learning experience for children to teach them about lone cetaceans. Ideally, the project will serve as a means to transbond and share mythic stories of lone cetaceans throughout the world. Humans could then align their personal mythology with passion and a goal of living without harm to the cetacean by avoiding any real-time contact with the whales and dolphins in captivity.

I am challenged by skeptics who ask me, "What's the point? How can a whale love?" I say, "With that magnificent brain and beautiful heart, how could they not?" Seeing the perspective of whales and dolphins as best I can is my life's work. We need to understand that the trans-species perception is not just our own - loving with the other's eye is the true meaning of unconditional love.

Thoughts from Caroline

We all have personas we embrace. Sometimes we are a business executive or a mother or a volunteer. But, in every moment, we are more than any persona or any label. We have a divine soul at our core, and that soul is at all times capable of reaching out to another soul. We always have an option to send unconditional love to the world. There is no moment, ever, when we cannot send our love to someone or something. We always have the power to heal.

Affirmation

We can always find ways to love.

Everyone comes to Santa Claus to make requests for Christmas. Of course, Santa knows he can't make promises to the children who visit him. After all, he needs to check inventory at the North Pole, confer with his elves to see if they have certain items, and, of course, check his "naughty and nice" book.

I was offered my first job as a "real Santa Claus" outside of a local Wal-Mart store on a cold December night. As I stood in front of the store and rang my bell for the Salvation Army, a lady stopped at my kettle and said, "You are the most real looking Santa Claus I have ever seen!" I thanked her and told her I appreciated the compliment. She then asked if I made calls on company and private Christmas parties. I told her I hadn't, but I would certainly like to do so! Since that night, I've had many chances to visit with that woman and her employees.

My visit in 2002 was especially memorable. I arrived early so I decided to have dinner with everyone. As I walked in, I saw a little boy at the buffet whose plate was full of nothing but shredded cheese. He asked if I could help him so I began to talk with him. I asked him if he liked cheese and if that was all he planned to eat. He told me his name was Jeffrey, and he invited me to sit at his table with his family. When I agreed, he escorted me to the head of his table, and then took me back to the serving line, where he described how good everything was as he filled my plate with food. He even told me how good green beans were for me - but that he didn't like them!

After he escorted me back to the table, Jeffrey politely helped me off with my coat and placed it over the back of my chair, like a little valet. I took my gloves off while he held my chair for me to sit down. As we sat at the dinner table together, he asked all sorts of questions about my reindeer and the North Pole and Mrs. Claus. He asked so many questions that his grandmother finally had to tell him to, "Let Santa finish his dinner, Jeffrey."

After a wonderful dinner, Jeffrey helped me put my jacket back on along with my gloves and hat. Then, he led me to my chair, next to a big, beautiful Christmas tree. As he helped me get situated, all of the children came and crowded around us. Jeffrey asked me if he could be first, and I told him that I didn't know whose present was whose, and he would have to wait his turn as I called out the names. I did tell him he could be Santa's special helper, since he knew all of the children and could help me find them to give them their gift and listen to their Christmas list.

One by one, I called the children up to receive their present from Santa. Young children as well as the older ones were delighted when they sat on Santa's knee and told him what they wanted for Christmas. Then, as Santa handed them their present, they would gleefully unwrap the gift to take home with them. There must have been twenty-five children!

I could tell Jeffrey was getting nervous that there might not be a present for him, but he remained patient. He would offer me a drink of water from time to time and would carefully put the glass on the table next to my chair. Each time another child's name was called he would enthusiastically announce their name to the crowd.

Finally, there was only one present left. Jeffrey looked concerned that the package might not be for him. I slowly picked up the package, looked all over it for his name, and found it! I had begun to wonder what in the world I would say if it was not for him! When I called his name, he literally jumped into my lap. He was so relieved that Santa had not forgotten him!

As I had done with each child, I asked Jeffrey what he would like for Santa to bring him for Christmas. He told me all he wanted was a fire truck. We began to talk about all of the fire trucks I have at the North Pole and what specific kind he wanted. "I want a remote control fire truck with a ladder that goes up," he replied. I told him I would see what I could do, thanked him for being such a great host and helper, and then slid him off of my lap so that he could open his present. As he began to tear the wrappings from the package that was nearly as big as he was, what should appear but the biggest, shiniest, remote control fire truck I had ever seen!

Jeffrey squealed with delight as he ran back to me, threw his arms around my neck, and said, "You did it! You brought me just what I wanted! You knew it all of the time! Thank you, thank you, and thank you!"

I was as surprised and delighted as he was!

What a wonderful gift that was for me because, you see, I don't believe in coincidences. My role as Santa Claus was authenticated in my own heart, as I believe God quickly wrapped that last package with exactly the toy he requested. I believe God led me to Jeffrey that night because He knew what a special little fellow he was and that he was in need of a sign of unconditional love. And, on that night, Jeffrey needed a reason, a sign, to believe in Santa Claus … and so did Santa!

As I have grown in my role as Santa, I have decided there really isn't a "naughty and nice" list. I believe in my heart that to Santa, all children who still believe in him belong on the nice list. For that reason, I carry a little, red book with me in which I write down the names of children who visit me and a word or two about what they request for Christmas.

Over the years, the list of names in my "Santa's Book" has grown. Often children want to know if their names are in Santa's Book so together we will look for them. Their eyes light up as they intently search the pages looking for their own names. If after a few pages we don't find them, I just tell them I will have to write them in, and then, with pen in hand, I let them tell me what their names are and what they want for Christmas. I can see and feel the sense of security it gives the children knowing their names are in Santa's Book.

During one special visit with children, a young lad who was about seven years old hung to the back of the line until he was sure he would have a private audience with Santa Claus. After he climbed on to my lap, we exchanged the usual greetings, and then I asked him what he would like for Christmas. He surprised me when he told me he didn't want anything for Christmas. Then, he pulled me to him so he could whisper in my ear.

"All I want for Christmas is for the rest of the children in my school to quit picking on me and calling me names."

My heart instantly broke. I had felt the same way when I was his age, and the memories of the pain it had caused came flooding back. It broke again when I realized this child believed I could change his circumstances. I knew there was no way I could make the children quit making fun of him – that was a promise Santa could not make.

I said, "I understand how you feel, son, but Santa can't be with you all of the time when other children are picking on you, and I'm afraid that Santa can't make them stop. I can make you a promise, though. I am going to write your name in my book, and, when I get home tonight, I will say my prayers for you."

A warm smile came over the young man's face as he meekly replied, "O.K" That was all he had to tell me so I gave him a big hug, and he was on his way.

Just as he left my lap, I felt the Holy Spirit speak to me: "That is a promise you can keep, Santa!" So that night, when I got home after a long day's work, I took out my Santa's Book, turned to the page with the young lad's name on it, and began to talk to God about his request. I sent all of my love to him, and to myself, for the suffering we had shared.

In that moment, I felt as if all of heaven opened up. As I talked, I felt like every angel was listening to my request. I knew in my heart that my prayers for this boy were being heard. That is when I realized I could use my role as Santa Claus to send unconditional love to all children, to be a living example of it, to portray unconditional love on their level, and show them it is possible.

I have entered many names and circumstances into what I now call "Santa's Prayer Book." I even have a special pocket sewn into my coat where I carry it. Each name and request is important and represents a special visit that I have had with precious children. The book represents the privilege I have to "keep Santa's promise" to pray for the special names and requests hidden in its pages. I now realize that when I pray for those children I may be the only person who has ever lifted their name to heaven. What an awesome privilege Santa has to represent such precious children, and what confidence I now have that there is one promise Santa can keep!

At Christmas time, I often find myself caught up in the excitement of my role as Santa Claus, while knowing full well I can't grant everyone's wish - or even anyone's. At those times, I reach back into my memory and into my heart and realize I can give the gift of unconditional love to everyone I meet. I can rely on my own faith in God and humankind, and I can try to impart that faith to others. I can share the gift of hope, both for myself and our world, and show that these priceless gifts are the greatest of all.

After all, it was Christ himself who said, "Faith, hope, and love, these three remain. But the greatest of these is love."

Thoughts from Caroline

Harboring guilt is one of our most destructive tendencies. When we are able to understand that everything happens for a reason, we can then validate its gift to our lives. And, from that validation, we can act. We can share our knowledge with others, and we can spread the lesson we have learned. All has reason. Nothing is ever in vain. We can be thankful we are blessed with the ability to share with others our newfound knowledge.

Affirmation

We are all loved, and we all can love.

There was a time when I hated myself. If you had asked one of my peers or the generations ahead of me if they thought I was happy, they would have told you I had a nice smile. I had not witnessed this for myself. It wasn't until my early thirties that I actually ever looked at myself in the mirror or allowed anyone to snap a photo of me. The kind of self-hate that I harbored was my secret, not to be shown to the outside world. I could have blamed it on the way certain people treated me when I was young, but, instead, I blamed it on myself.

I was born like everyone else, with a gift. My gift is that not only can I talk to animals and have them understand me, but they also can talk back and I understand them. I grew up on a 14-acre farm with horses, ponies, cats, rabbits, a dog, and a parakeet. It was a beautiful life most of the time. Some nights I would fall asleep elated by the connections and experiences I shared with the animals. I didn't understand that no one else could hear the animals the way I could so on many nights I tossed in terror of what people knowingly put animals through. It was a time when people swatted and kicked dogs for having diarrhea in the house, beat horses for refusing jumps, and declawed cats for scratching the furniture.

My teenage comments of, "Jinx, the dog, is sick because he ate something the farrier left down at the barn. Cali, my horse, is not jumping because her hip is hurting her, and Samantha, the cat, wonders why she can't live in the house anymore," went completely unnoticed. I was never told I was not hearing them, but I was often told I was "too sensitive" and had an "active imagination."

Despite all of this, I was a child filled with joy. It was when I was 15 years old that my unconditional love for the world and for myself turned to disgust. My best friend, my horse Excalibur, was sent away to a horse dealer at my trainer's request. She had decided that

Excalibur was no longer good enough for me and that she must be replaced. I fought to keep Excalibur, but no one listened.

In the months that followed, I had vision after vision of Excalibur being beaten, starved, and in pain. When she came back to the farm for a few days, she arrived an exhausted and defeated horse. She tried hard to be perfect, and I begged for her to be allowed to stay, but they sent her away. Not long after that, I quit riding horses. I could no longer look the other animals in the eye. I was embarrassed that I had allowed Excalibur to be sent away and to be mistreated by strangers. I parted from the animals in the barn in shame.

Without horses in my life, I found it hard to put my heart into anything. I played sports but didn't care if we won. I became a hippie, went to college, studied biology and animal rights, began to meditate, read books on spirituality, took classes in energy healing, worked at a flower farm and at a Montessori school, ran a pet-sitting/dog-walking business and wondered, "What the hell am I going to do with the rest of my life?" Although it may have appeared I had passions for many things, I had no passion for anything. There were times when I didn't even want to get out of bed.

In my early twenties, I took a class in "animal communication." When I arrived home that evening, I asked my dog Lala how she was doing. I clearly heard her tell me, "Mom, I am dying inside." I took a breath and asked again. Again, the voice in my head repeated, "Mom, I am dying inside." At the time, I did not notice anything physically wrong with Lala. My boyfriend urged me to put aside what I had heard and labeled it paranoia. Two months later, Lala died of cancer.

At the moment of Lala's death, I felt her spirit engulf me, wrap around me like a warm Caribbean day breeze, and tingle like the beginning of a tickle. I saw the atmosphere in front of me change. Her spirit around me looked like golden coins at the bottom of a wishing well or bright yellow Aspen leaves covered in morning dew, flickering in the sunlight. My heart felt no pain, just pure unconditional love for everything around me. I was already convinced there was a God, but this experience convinced me that

God loves the world's creatures.

But, I was still not convinced God loved me.

In 1997, I rescued Maia. She was eighteen months old, tall, lanky, big-pawed, beautiful, and part German Shepherd. Mine was her fourth home. Maia was aggressive with people and other dogs. She had separation anxiety and had been beaten so badly she suffered with migraines and saw three of everything all her life. It took me two years to find out that Maia was 98 percent wolf. I had been told by many trainers to put her to sleep or confine her to the yard. When I first adopted Maia, I asked a pioneering animal communicator to talk to her because I was only a beginner. She told me Maia was too wild and couldn't receive anything from her telepathically.

For many years, life seemed to get harder. Maia's behavior frequently brought me to tears. I always talked about what I couldn't do. I couldn't go to the dog park or the beach on a crowded day. I couldn't trust her around children or elders. I couldn't tie her outside the coffee shop. I couldn't even leave the car windows open for her in a parking lot. Not only did I have to keep Maia safe, but I also had to keep others safe from her. I had to be quick and alert at all times.

Despite Maia's unruliness, she had the compassion of a saint. Any given day, I could be hiding from her wild, sharp teeth while wedged between the refrigerator and the wall, then tackling her as she went after a small dog, then curling up with her in the evening, as she gently licked my arm while our bunny rested on her back.

I watched in awe as she battled and survived cancer and Rocky Mountain Spotted Fever. I saw her struggle with trying to tame her wolf nature and become more civilized. As Maia and my animal family aged, I witnessed her becoming more and more conscious. By the time of her passing, she had children and elderly human friends. She had learned to stop herself from attacking small dogs when they ran within striking distance, and she often asked me to relay her wise insights to my friends.

Maia had been with me most of my adult life. Who I am today

has its roots in what I have learned from being Maia's person. It is because of Maia that I became a pet psychic and animal trainer. I've helped thousands of animals become non-aggressive, confident, and understood because of my experiences with Maia.

We've hiked in the wildest of backcountry. She has saved me from at least three mountain lion attacks. Maia taught me to read the signs of the presence of animals in the wilderness, how to read animal behavior, and the importance of teaching animals to communicate with each other. I have learned that a wolf hybrid still lives by wolf rhythms, even though their people do not realize it. I have learned that animals forgive us when we falter. I have learned that they see and appreciate how hard we try to be good and to survive in a world with so many contradictions. They love us without conditions.

After my experience with Excalibur, I had harbored a guilt and shame that haunted me throughout my life. This shame paralyzed me and crippled me into believing I was not worthy of enjoying life. My love for Maia and her unconditional love for me healed me of this. I believe Maia was God's gift to me to recover and forgive myself. Rescuing, rehabilitating, and loving Maia unconditionally taught me to be self-assured. I needed to learn to stand tall, to lift my head up, and be firm in my voice and in my convictions.

I needed to believe in my heart that I could actually make a difference if I persevered. I believe a higher power presented me with such a difficult test so I could internalize all of Maia's and my accomplishments.

I learned to fail and then to get up and start anew each day. I learned that each failure made me more conscious of who I am and what paths lead to success. I learned that my voice does matter and that I am here on earth to educate society on the vastness of the world's animal consciousness.

Because I feel so passionately about my love for the animals and my role as their voice, I have learned to look in the mirror and care about my appearance. I have begun to enjoy smiling. If we love our animals unconditionally, we learn to love ourselves unconditionally as well.

Very often our animals are our mirrors. As we strive to help them overcome their fears and their aggressions, we learn to overcome our fears and take control of our impulsive acts. We learn that each body movement and each thought creates a ripple effect, either positive or negative. We can choose to persevere and highlight our successes, or we can choose to wallow in guilt and shame and stay stagnant in our lives.

I have learned that a higher power loves each and every one of us and wants us to be happy. I have learned that this higher power masks opportunities for growth and discovering our gifts by concealing them in hardships and frustrations. Excalibur, Maia, and all the other animals in my life have taught me to relax, take a breath, think of my own behavior, my own words, and my own struggles, and then look at other beings with compassion.

I tell the animals that the smartest ones are conscious of their behavior in each moment. We must know what we are doing at every moment and why. By doing so, we begin to communicate more clearly with one another. Not only do we begin to love others more fully and more deeply, but we also begin to love ourselves more profoundly. When we feel the exchange of unconditional love with our animals, we learn to love ourselves unconditionally.

Thoughts from Caroline

Perhaps the most profound element of unconditional love is the development of unconditional love for ourselves. We may think, "Who am I to be proud of my accomplishments when others have done more?" Or, "Who am I to enjoy an expensive meal when so many others are starving?" We can even convince ourselves, "I am not valuable enough" to take care of my body, or put my needs first, or take a needed time-out. God didn't make just some souls valuable and loveable – we are *all* in His image. It is essential we honor God's wisdom and learn to value and love ourselves.

Affirmation

I deserve unconditional love as I am, now.

Gloria Tom Wing Staudt

author of "Live Your Vacation: The Ultimate Guide to Live Your Dream Life ... Every Day!" and founder of Peak Success Coaching

"Begin with the end in mind" – Stephen Covey

A more peaceful and loving world is the vision I hold dearly. A path to that end, of a more peaceful and loving world, is to give ourselves and others unconditional love. This is the most powerful gift we can give. We have all had at least one experience that involved unconditional love, a moment that left us with a deep desire to give and receive more of this precious gift every day.

Unconditional love observed

"Intense love does not measure, it just gives" – Mother Teresa

Some of my fondest memories are of the unconditional love I observed as a child. My immigrant parents were from China but lived in Trinidad, a West Indian island in the Caribbean. Every Christmas, they prepared several full cartons of gifts, all food products, that Papa delivered personally with no expectations of "getting" anything back. These gifts were their gesture of appreciation of each person/family in our lives, and there was pure joy to give, a feeling and value I live today.

As a chef, Papa believed meals were best served alongside friends. Any time he cooked, he would invite numerous people to join us. He often made each of our favorite dishes, and whenever he cooked a special meal, he would put aside a box of each dish for our uncle with polio, who lived alone in the countryside. I often went along for the ride to deliver these meals. Little did I know consciously that I was learning what unconditional love looked like and how much I would value it in my life.

As a teenager, not understanding my much older dad, I learned that love can be expressed in different ways than we might expect. I recognized that one expression of Papa's unconditional love was putting aside food for me when I was out volunteering at church – even though he was displeased that I was not home helping Mama with the bakery business. Our relationship was transformed, and I felt the love I had observed and knew the joy in my whole being. Mama lovingly sending Papa off with a silent prayer for his safety each time he went out, and loving him, no matter how long he was away from home – that was unconditional love I noticed and treasured. These observations of unconditional love contributed to the safe and joyful feelings I had growing up.

Divinely guided outward & giving to others

"You make a living by what you get. You make a life by what you give." – Winston Churchill

As I reflect upon my life, one of the crystal clear memories of divine guidance was a profound sense of responsibility to shift people's perception toward the truth and away from racial labeling. This sense of responsibility came during my teenage years in the 1960s. While I was growing up in Trinidad, I volunteered at my church to be on the team of Sunday church service readers. I knew that my purpose to read in public was to be a positive role model of "Chinese people."

This was not because I experienced any racial tensions; in fact my closest high school friends were from diverse ethnic backgrounds and we saw each other not as our racial backgrounds, but as friends who ate lunch together, went on school trips together, and had fun. Looking back, I saw it then as an inner knowledge. Today, I see it as divine guidance. That was the start of my journey of volunteering, giving of my talents for the good of others. Giving to others, I discovered, was a source of joy.

When I moved to New York to go to university, I began another phase of my life. Being educated, living, working, and getting married in New York was another level of evolution and foundation building. My learning and experiences there were preparing me for the next phase of life in Canada as a mother, conscious entrepreneur, and volunteer in various school, church, business, and Rotary groups. I gave unconditionally in meaningful ways because of divine guidance, amidst many who did not understand fully, yet supported me in various ways. That took courage, conviction, faith, trust, and unconditional love from family and friends.

Consciously going inward

"Love is all you need" – John Lennon

Loving myself unconditionally required conscious effort. I did not wake up one day and decide to love myself unconditionally. Like most, if asked, "Do you love yourself?" I would have answered, "Yes, of course I do." However, actually getting there was an evolutionary journey.

The crystal clear catalyst of my first gift of unconditional love to myself was when I gave myself permission to stop pushing myself so hard to be worthy of being called a coach and to take ten minutes of "Be still & do nothing" time in nature. I am dedicated to giving unconditionally to family, business, and community, but what was missing was slowing down and giving to myself. Transformation began and grew into taking pampering baths for 30 minutes to an hour. Previously, that would have been inconceivable in my go-go life, which was built on the productive fast pace of doing, doing, doing.

Self-Mastery – Win for all

Another significant part of my gift of unconditional love to myself was my commitment to invest in my inward journey. The resulting gifts were a rediscovery of who I am, a discovery of what wellness means to me, and the commitment to share what I know about the power of forgiveness and letting go.

One of the most significant shifts in my relationship with my husband came when through my coach, Jean Pierre LeBlanc, I saw the blessings of all that was challenging in our relationship. Once I remembered and knew without any doubt and with firm conviction who I was, life became more effortless, and it became easier to love myself unconditionally.

It was always easy for me to love others unconditionally. Now, I also am a master at loving myself unconditionally. By doing so, I feel confident in pursuing higher purposes for myself and for the good of all. At this level, I look for what to celebrate and what to do:

to be compassionate;
to more quickly get back on track when I allow myself to get off track;
to take full responsibility for my part in any situation;
to look for the blessings in disguise;
to risk being vulnerable;
to ask for help without attachment to the outcome and graciously and gratefully receive help given to me;
to joyfully celebrate others' successes;
to follow divine guidance;
to continue to have faith and trust in my divine journey unfolding as it is meant;
to love unconditionally.

Inherent paradoxes

A point to note is the discernment of the truth in apparent paradoxes. For example, because of my personal high standards of excellence, I am conscious of discerning the paralyzing impact of being a perfectionist, versus the thought of lowering my standards. Taking a closer look to clarify and confirm that you are not lowering your standards but, rather, letting go of being a perfectionist, places you at ease and gives you the choice to love unconditionally in your decisions and actions. What guides and energizes me is that my motivation comes from a pure knowledge of who I am and from my desire for the good of all in my daily experiences.

Pursuing Higher Purpose

"We must be the change we wish to see in the world" – *Mahatma Ghandi*

Loving yourself unconditionally is not a destination. It is a journey to be lived with mastery. What I have found is that as I love myself unconditionally, I consciously choose to be free of the hold distractions have on me. I am free to live fully present with joy and to shine brilliantly, to choose to be my highest and best self, to love others unconditionally, and to meet them wherever they are.

I also notice that I live each day with more ease and grace, as if my life is one long vacation. This stage of consciousness – living with unconditional love – is where I am and what I want for others. I am also a lifelong learner. With an open mind and open heart, I approach each day with deep gratitude for all my blessings and a curiosity toward all that evolves.

Celebrating and Inspiring

We can all celebrate each other and be inspired to do our part to heal our planet and enjoy a more peaceful and loving world. In doing so, we will leave a legacy of unconditional love, where loving others as ourselves and honoring life is the golden rule. Follow your intuition to decide what action resonates for your highest good.

Thoughts from Caroline

Each moment presents an opportunity to experience unconditional love. Even a seemingly mundane encounter can have profound significance when we step outside of our boxes and see the encounter as one between souls. What message would our soul choose to offer? What might we learn from this person, who, from a human perspective, may be judged as having little to offer? It is up to us to capture the importance of each moment and allow our souls to heal each other.

Affirmation

I recognize the potential for love in each moment.

Most of us have heard of the concept of mindfulness. We often hear it explained in terms such as concentration, Dhyana, presence, silence, etc. The terminology can be quite cold and sterile at times.

Pure mindfulness, however, is the same as pure love and pure presence. The ego pushes away uncomfortable experience and clings to comfortable experience. This creates tension within us and between us. When we are present with moment-to-moment experience, however, we embody love.

I spent four years working at gas stations. One night, on the graveyard shift, a man walked in and asked to use the phone. He had a very hardened, "ghetto" type of personality. The phone inside was broken and so was the payphone. When he found this out, he fiercely cussed me out. I was not too phased, as these things happen in gas stations, but the situation was very intense. Rather than resent the man and the situation, I decided to view it as an invitation to cultivate mindfulness.

I gathered up as much consciousness and inner strength as possible. I built up a solid sense of presence through diaphragmatic breathing. I felt my feet on the ground and was present with the experience in the moment.

When the proper level of mindfulness manifested itself, I calmly explained to him that it was a matter beyond my control. My explanation wasn't good enough. He continued with abusive language and walked toward the door.

Over the years, I had learned that the best thing to do, normally, was to let an angry person walk out the door. However, my new-found sense of presence allowed me access to "the still-soft voice," which told me that there was unfinished business. I called after him. I don't remember what I said, but he didn't like it.

The man stopped at the door, turned around, came back to the counter, and stared me down with a look of death. I continued with the mindfulness practice.

It became apparent that every conflict occurs to clear a tension point in the body-mind. The aggressor approaches with a tension point that is similar to yours or similar and opposite. As a personality, they have come to "hurt" you. As a soul, they have come to heal you.

I felt the presence of this man "burn" through my weakness. The weakness was felt in my throat chakra and other places in the body-mind. It became apparent that he was teaching me presence and assertiveness. He was very assertive but in an unbalanced and aggressive way. He had a fear of getting the short end of the stick in life. Therefore, his weakness was similar but opposite to mine. Mine was passive. His was aggressive.

The only way to heal this man was to heal my own weakness. When this became apparent, all tension dissolved. This allowed me to work with the reality of the moment and to handle the confrontation in a way that mirrored his stern demeanor. I made a very clear case, in a rather assertive and stern manner, about my lack of control over the phone situation and about my right to respect as a human being. The case was made without the desire to make him wrong. This actually melted my weakness and provided him with an opportunity to allow his weakness to settle.

In that moment, I felt that the man healed me. I then offered him a free drink: an offering of appreciation. Immediately, his weakness dissolved, and his heart opened to me. He fought back tears as he realized I was sincere. All he could say was, "You a good person. You a good person."

When we practice the art of presence in a conflict and clear the weakness the antagonist is unconsciously trying to heal, then we automatically clear the other person's weakness. There is a mirror-like or boomerang-like process that occurs. I call this, "The Droopy Effect," which is named after the cartoon character.

Meditation trains the mind to be present with ALL experience as it rises into consciousness. When you apply this to interpersonal relationships, miracles tend to happen. When you resent an experience with another human being, you push away the experience and create a polarization. This creates increased separation rather than communion, which is a reflection of the oneness of all life.

We later went out for a cigarette. He told me that, at one point, he thought I was going to take out a gun and shoot him. That was because I was mirroring his aggression without any aggression inside of me.

Afterward, he left, and I continued to work my shift. We slipped back into our mundane routines.

There is nothing special about what I did that night. With ongoing training in mindfulness and regular reminders of the oneness of all life, we can all accomplish true miracles in situations that we normally think of as bad. It simply requires ongoing practice to prepare ourselves for such moments.

Mindfulness is unconditional love. The two are inseparable.

Thoughts from Caroline

When we are called to be a support system for someone, the greatest gift we can provide them is unconditional space – a space where we are not offended, a space where we do not ignite further controversy, a space where we do not act as an injured party, a space where we do not encourage their guilt for certain behaviors. In a challenging situation with another, we can put aside our ego and meet them with our soul. We can choose to provide them the room they need to grow.

I exercise patience with myself and others in my pursuit of unconditional love.

Love Like God

Tom Wright

former presidential aide, author of eight books, and coursework creator of "The One Penny Millionaire! ®" online seminar and the "A Course In Shamanism ®" online seminar

The moment my daughter turned fourteen, I no longer knew her. The daughter I had was gone. Without a moment's notice, she disappeared, and there was someone new in her body. What I didn't know at first was that she didn't know who she was either.

I didn't realize the full extent of the change until it came time for our annual trip to Disney World. Every summer, we would gleefully embark on our trip filled with anticipation and fueled by plenty of ice cream. Then, all of a sudden, I was the enemy, not to be hugged or held hands with in public. There was no Disney. No ice cream. Few smiles. And *no* hugs anymore, even at home. I was stunned. What did I do? And, more importantly, what could I do to fix it?

I was terrified that our relationship would never go back to the loving hugs-and-kisses dream it once was. I wondered whether she would ever look up to me again, or if we could laugh together anymore. I was scared, and I didn't know how to handle it. It seemed all we could do was fight, though neither of us could ever remember what the fight was about. In those tense moments, it seemed our lives hung in the balance. And, the tension lasted for a long, long, time.

Car rides were often the worst. I would drive, not knowing what to say or whether I should say anything at all, and she would sit with her earbuds in, purposefully oblivious. I would worry that anything I said would only lead to more resentment, more shouting. That any attempt at conversation would only leave us more alienated and further apart from each other than ever. Yet, I had to say something to the new person I was living with so I would try.

There was a time when I believed, "I love you," those three little words that used to bring a smile to her face without fail, would heal just about anything. I soon learned I was wrong. When hormones rage, social pressures push, and the imagination runs wild, those three little words don't seem to fix much anymore. Somehow the pathway from the ears to the heart gets blocked.

I tried my best to be loving, to be sensitive. I tried to react with reason rather than anger. But, everything I did only added to her frustration. Every word out of my mouth aggravated her further. What was I supposed to do? Why wasn't there a parenting manual that could teach me how to reach her?

If I claimed to understand, I only made matters worse. I was very quickly told that I was *not* a teenage girl and so I could *not* know what was going on with her. Truth was, I didn't. So, after a prolonged battle over that one, and a new realization for me, I gave it up, gave in, and told her that, in fact, how could I know what was going on with her, since I never *had* been a teenage girl? And, that from the looks of how it was going for her, I lucked out on that one!

My admission seemed to open a small doorway in our communication, which I was determined to walk through with more than merely those first few words. But the doorway was so small. I couldn't fit all I had to say through it all at once.

Even now, there are many times when I have to pick my words carefully. And, I have to make sure that the environment we communicate within is a safe one for her. Thanks to that one tiny breakthrough, I have hopes there will be more. Anger can be handled, slammed doors tolerated in a fashion, but to be cut off altogether is unthinkable. Not impossible, just unthinkable.

In an effort to learn from other parents who had been through their child's teenage years and lived to tell the tale, I jumped at any chance for conversation. I learned that parents often can't stop talking about the perils of the teen years, even if their kids are in their thirties. The memories they have of what they went through are as fresh as the day they happened. I heard heartening tales of grown children who thanked their parents for standing strong, offering guidance, and being there when they were needed. I heard it was hard, and they did the best they could. I heard them admit they weren't perfect. I heard them say it would pass, and that, finally, after years of struggle, I would hear the three words I longed to hear: "Daddy, I love you." I heard all of that, but I never heard the most important lesson of all. It took an article on a website, written by a teenage girl, to finally teach me what every parent around me had been saying, the truly important message that I had failed to grasp: *It wasn't personal.*

In the article, the girl expressed regret for how she had once acted, for the things that she had said, for becoming so angry at her parents for things that now seemed so harmless. As I read her list of the various ways in which her father had once offended her, I could do nothing but laugh out loud as I recognized each and every one of them. Her words encouraged me and offered me strength. I finally knew that we would make it through this!

I felt a deep love and compassion for that girl and her courage, for what she had given me. This wasn't a light at the end of the tunnel; this was the light *in* the tunnel. The light that would allow me to see past the overreactions that come too strongly from feeling blamed and shut out to the open acceptance that comes from knowing my daughter's outbursts are not about me, even if it feels that way.

Now, whenever I look over at her, I know that she is still in there somewhere, just as scared as I am, and unable or unwilling to ask for the comfort and support she so desperately needs. I know that she still loves me. Sometimes, I can even see it in her eyes.

I wish I could say at this point that our struggles are far behind us, but they're not. I am still the father of a teenage girl, which means at least another two years of hormones, social pressure, and upset to go through. For now, I'll have to find my joy in whatever time we spend together and in being there for her as much as I can.

I know this will pass, and I look forward to the day my little girl, as a beautiful, balanced young woman, goes from feeling love behind the tears that come so often these days to telling me once again that she, too, loves her Daddy. In the meantime, with open arms and a wide heart, I'll be right here, waiting for her, with tears in my eyes, too.

Closing Thoughts

Reading "Love Like God" has pushed you to rethink and redefine the love in your life. This is good. Begin here. You have discovered a starting point to a life filled with love that is true, love that is unconditional. Embrace it in all its joy and freedom, and celebrate this return to the pureness of your heart!

Remember:

All is love.

You are loved.

I love you.

Please share this message and this book with others.

Blessings,
Caroline A. Shearer

Quotes to Inspire Unconditional Love

"Even after all this time, the sun never says to the earth, 'You owe me.' Look what happens with a love like that. It lights the whole sky." ~ *Hafez of Shiraz*

"Where you find no love, put love -- and you will find love." ~ *John of the Cross.*

"Love is life. All, everything that I understand, I understand only because I love. Everything is, everything exists, only because I love. Everything is united by it alone." ~ *Leo Tolstoy*

"To love for the sake of being loved is human, but to love for the sake of loving is angelic." ~ *Alphonse de Lamartine*

"The beginning of love is to let those we love be perfectly themselves, and not to twist them to fit our own image. Otherwise, we love only the reflection of ourselves we find in them." ~ *Thomas Merton*

"Your task is not to seek for love, but merely to seek and find all the barriers within yourself that you have built against it." ~ *Rumi*

"You, yourself, as much as anybody in the entire universe, deserve your love and affection." ~ *Buddha*

Mother Teresa

"I have found the paradox, that if you love until it hurts, there can be no more hurt, only more love."

"The success of love is in the loving - it is not in the result of loving. Of course it is natural in love to want the best for the other person, but whether it turns out that way or not does not determine the value of what we have done."

"If you judge people, you have no time to love them."

"Intense love does not measure, it just gives."

Appendix

Contributor Bios

Portia "Lady Rerun" Berry Allen is the daughter of popular dance and television legend Fred "Rerun" Berry of the 1970's NBC sitcoms, "What's Happening" and "What's Happening Now." As an African-American female, wife, and mother of three, Allen is an accomplished actress, radio and television personality, celebrity speaker/hostess, and a plus-size model. Aside from pursuing her dreams of entertainment, she is an active supporter of the Autism Foundation, as two of her children have been diagnosed with autism. She is a role model to the youth in her community, and she believes in networking with new people to continually open herself to new opportunities. www.ladyrerun.com

Father of five, dean of students for the New York City Department of Education for over 12 years, and a Christian, **K.L. Belvin** is the co-founder of Bravin Publishing LLC, a literary publishing company geared toward publishing authors who present minorities as role models for today's youth. In June 2008, Keith released his first manuscript, "A Man in Transition," a book of poems, stories, and personal observations. Keith credits his enormous success to God and his wife, who also serves as his best friend. **Tiffany Braxton Belvin**, a native New Yorker, began performing in amateur fashion shows in the early 1990s. Tiffany began her professional career as one of the first signature models for the e-zine, Belle-Noir.com. Tiffany has appeared in various media outlets, including: "The Tyra Banks Show," ABC's "Eyewitness News," NBC's "Today" in New York, and Lifetime Television's "How to Look Good Naked." She is also the executive producer for The Miss Black Queens NY USA Pageant. She started Bravin Publishing with her husband and serves as its creative director. She is the author of, "Stop Doggy Posing! A Woman's Guide to Regaining Her Dignity in Relationships." www. bravinpublishing.com

The son of a pastor, **Jesse Birkey** grew up in the church with an intellectual knowledge of God. As a teenager, he faced the same struggles as everyone else, especially in the area of acceptance. He married his school sweetheart, made a career as a firefighter/

paramedic, and had two beautiful children. His life was enviable, and he found security in what he had until God allowed his most treasured relationship, his marriage, to be tested. The veil was pulled back, and he was able to see himself as he was: "poor, blind, and naked." He came to the revelation that he needed a relationship with God and not a religion. He made a choice to sacrifice his own selfish desires and walk in obedience to God. God restored his marriage and started him on a journey of understanding true love and intimacy. God has given Jesse a ministry of setting the captives free through Jesus Christ. He is the founder of Reflect Ministries and author of "Marriage What's the Point?" His website, www. marriagewhatsthepoint.com, is an outreach for the hurting and broken.

Chase Block is a15-year-old high school student. His parents divorced when he was five, and his experiences made him want to help other kids understand what to expect when their parents split. The day before he started his book, Chase's mom committed suicide, a move that shocked and devastated the community. Instead of shelving the project, Chase felt renewed urgency to share his personal journey from devastation to hope. How can kids handle thoughts of suicide, guilt about divorce, addiction, and emotional turmoil? Chase covers it all, and also lets them know when and where to reach out for help in "Chasing Happiness: One Boy's Guide to Helping Other Kids Cope with Divorce, Parental Addictions and Death." www.chaseblockbook.com

Anicia Bragg grew up in a small, southern town with big-city dreams of becoming a successful image consultant, designer, and mentor to children and young adults. Those dreams became a reality at an early age for Anicia when she landed a position as a spokesmodel for Eastman Kodak in her early twenties. Today, she is in high demand as an image consultant and collaborates with some of the most talented designers and professionals in the industry. As founder of a special events/production company and a designer, Anicia has coordinated celebrity galas, VIP parties, weddings, and award ceremonies. www.indulgewithaniciab.com

Kundan Chhabra has never had a girlfriend so he has learned to experience love no matter what. His experiences led him to develop a path toward wisdom and enlightenment, which he has shared through poems, stories, and articles about love that empower people in all relationships. Kundan is the author of, "Why I Don't Need You But I Want You Around Anyway" and "Experiencing Divinity, Sharing Awakening." His upcoming book is called, "Why I Have Never Paid for a First Date." Through his commitment to the experience of divinity and his desire to share awakening, Kundan has helped many people feel loved, joyful, and clear. He can be reached at www.whyareyousolovable.com/blog.html.

Robin Craig, a native Houstonian, was in the National Honor Society and graduated from Aldine Senior High magna cum laude. She studied business administration and communications at Sam Houston State University in Huntsville, Texas, and graduated from Columbia School of Broadcasting. Robin worked as a radio deejay and television veejay on a live national music video station before moving to Nashville, Tennessee, where she hosted "Nashville Future Stars," "TV Swap Shop," and "TV Home Listings" and appeared in television commercials and music videos. She also worked as a casting director, location scout, and location manager for film and television. From 2001-2008, Robin worked as a producer for "Texas Justice," "Judge Alex," and "Cristina's Court," nationally syndicated court television shows owned by Twentieth Television, a division of Fox, and she won three national daytime Emmys (2008, 2009, 2010) in the category, "Outstanding Legal Courtroom Program." Lastly, Robin is a writer and motivational speaker who authors the "Today's Widow" segment for the Houston Chronicle and hosts "Robin Craig LIVE" on the Mingle Media Television Network. www.robincraigdirect.com

Crystal Dwyer's unique approach to success, along with her education and expertise in advanced hypnotherapy and life coaching, helps people achieve positive change in the shortest time. She has a burning desire to share these success principles with as many people as she can reach. Not only has she helped thousands understand how their own subconscious thought systems are what create either havoc or great success in their lives, her system successfully guides people to purge their "messy thinking" forever and create a life they love. Crystal is certified by the American Board of Hypnotherapy, is a Member of the International Coaching Federation, and is certified by the Chopra Center of Well-Being as a Meditation Instructor. Through Crystal's personal coaching, speaking, CD programs, videos, books, and articles, people all over the world have experienced profound and lasting transformation in relationships, career, health, and wellness. You can learn more about self-hypnosis and total life transformation on Crystal's website, www.crystalvisionlife.com.

Tonya Fitzpatrick, Esq., is an attorney, author, entrepreneur, speaker, sought-after travel expert, and the executive producer and co-host of the award-winning "World Footprints" radio show - a leader in socially conscious travel. Prior to her transition away from corporate America, Tonya received a political appointment to the U.S. Department of Education, where she served as a deputy assistant secretary, and was contracted to work as the senior legal advisor for the Office of Civil Rights at the U.S. Department of Homeland Security. Tonya has co-authored a new iPhone travel application entitled, "Baltimore & Beyond," is working on a second application called, "Global DC," and contributed a chapter in a book with Stephen Covey, Patricia Fripp, and Tony Alessandra entitled, "Success Simplified." Tonya graduated from the London School of Economics, East China University of Law and Politics, and Wayne State University Law School. She also won a fellowship at Michigan State University in the Michigan Political Leadership Program. Her greatest education, however, has come through traveling and sharing our world through "World Footprints." www.worldfootprints.com

Vida Ghaffari is active in the Tinseltown scene as an actress and a reporter. She has had three starring roles in cult filmmaker Joe Castro's well-regarded horror films and has starred in many other indie films. Vida has worked alongside well-known child stars, including, with Allison Arngrim (Nellie Oleson of "Little House on the Prairie") in "The Bilderberg Club" and with Jeremy Miller (Ben Seaver of "Growing Pains") in a television pilot. Ghaffari also played an Iraqi wife in Comedy Central's "Mind of Mencia." She made her comedic, web-series debuts in "Alternative Brother" and "Green Manor," alongside Tony Moran, the original Michael Myers from "Halloween." She has acted in plays at established Hollywood venues, such as the Zephyr Theatre and Theatre/Theater. Ghaffari is a voiceover artist for companies such as Fidelity Investments and is the voice of Singular Magazine. This multi-talented performer has worked as an entertainment correspondent, and she often reports from Hollywood, red-carpet film premieres, and galas, where she interviews a wide range of celebrities. Born and raised in the D.C. area, she comes from a long line of diplomats, scholars, actors/ directors, writers, and poets. Ghaffari wants to uphold the family tradition through the arts and the media. www.vidaghaffari.com

Lisa Gibson, executive director of the Peace & Prosperity Alliance, has a unique voice on global terrorism, having lost her brother in the 1988 terrorist bombing of Pan Am flight 103 over Lockerbie, Scotland. As a result of this tragedy, she overcomes evil with good by serving the people of Libya, the country found responsible for her brother's death. Her story of forgiveness made the headlines when she met with and forgave Libyan Leader Muammar Gaddafi, one of the world's most notorious terrorists and the man responsible for her brother's death. She has made it her life's mission to help others move through the pain of loss to wholeness and forgiveness and to prevent future acts of terror. Lisa is author of the award-winning book, "Life In Death: A Journey From Terrorism To Triumph" and the CD series, "Learning To Forgive: Your Pathway To Inner Peace." She has had guest appearances on CNN, ABC, CBS, MSNBC, and Kurdistan and Libyan Television, as well as having her story featured in USA Today, London Times, The New York Post, and countless others. During an interview with CNN, she was quoted as saying, "Love is the most effective weapon in the war on terrorism." www. peaceandprosperityalliance.org

Jon Graves is a former professional athlete and fitness diehard who now works for what he wants to believe is a quasi-government/secret service operation in San Diego, California. He is also co-founder of the single parent social network, SingleDad.com. His interests include politics, sports, television/film, and working with programs that support the needs of people dealing with cancer. Most important to him, though, is who he is as a man and father to the two most charming boys in the world. He's thrown pitches in Dodger Stadium, shared a Vegas elevator (and a very interesting conversation) with Tony Bennett, worked out with WWE Star The Undertaker, and had a burger with the founder of the Mexican Mafia. He's been involved in television pilots about single dads, was featured in a documentary film about marriage, and won the Game Show Network's popular dating show, "Baggage," in 2010. You can follow him online at JonGraves.com.

Gayle Gregory is the co-author of, "The Grand Experiment, an Expedition of Self Discovery" and author of the award-winning business management and leadership book, "Workplace Evolution: Common Sense for Uncommon Times." She is a former senior manager with two Fortune 500 companies and the founder of Pure Possibility, compassionate transitions coaching and mentoring. Gayle is also co-founder of Workplace Evolution. WE's coaching and facilitation services create a shift from "me" to "we" in the workplace that allows businesses to thrive in any climate. Her latest creative endeavor is as co-founder of The Institute for Bully Free Living, the face and voice of social courage. Gayle is an enlightening coach, a veteran of radio talk shows, and an inspirational and humorous, take-no-prisoners speaker. www.pure-possibility.org

Diana Harris is a nationally recognized intuitive counselor, psychic medium, and wisdom teacher. She is frequently sought after for the accuracy of her intuitive services, mediumship abilities, and dynamic workshops. Through her work, Diana inspires and leads those that she meets toward effecting positive and life-affirming changes in their lives. Her style is evocative of the well-known aphorism: "Know thyself and thou shalt know the world." Diana is often described as a bridge between the angelic and devic realm. She is a gifted clairaudient, clairvoyant, and clairsentient. Native American teachings, Huna, and shamanic traditions have been the primary focus of her spiritual path. Diana has a deep connection to Mother Earth, works with her Wisdom Keepers, and incorporates her knowledge of archetypes and earth medicine into her spiritual practice. She reaches audiences worldwide through her writing and radio engagements and travels throughout the U.S. to conduct workshops, speak at conferences, and offer intuitive counseling. Diana is a frequent contributing writer to "Kinetics," "SpiritSide," and other holistic journals. www.sacredspiraldance.com

Dana Heidkamp is a junior at the University of North Texas. She has always been a spiritual person, but her belief in unconditional love has turned her away from most organized religion. In 2008, while in her first year of college at a Baptist school, she decided to explore her faith more deeply. She was completely reborn and found her life significantly changed when she read the first of the "Conversations with God" series of books. Since then, she has spent as much time as possible spreading and reminding herself of its messages. Her trip to Kenya in 2009 further cemented her desire to change the world and help those in need. After she transferred universities, she switched her major to social work in hopes of experiencing her inner Divinity through service to others. She is excited to have her work included in such a beautiful collection.

At the age of sixteen, **Jennifer Hicks** had a surprising experience - she began knowing things before they happened! Her psychic ability accelerated: One night in college, as she walked home alone, she was jumped by a rapist. Her intuition gave her the information she needed to fight off her attacker and escape. Too fearful to let anyone know she had this gift, she kept it a secret from everyone. Years later, she began to spontaneously pick up psychic information that concerned criminal activity. With much apprehension, she went to the FBI, where she unexpectedly launched a career as a police psychic! Jennifer now reads for the public and can be heard weekly on her radio show, "Never a Dull Moment," where she does live readings on the air. Visit www.jenniferhicksmedium.com for more information.

Jennifer Hunt, a self-proclaimed "dream chaser," pursued her childhood passions for art, nature, and writing to adulthood. As a jewelry designer for her company, Jennifer Hunt Designs, and as a writer, poet, and columnist, she has been able to explore and tap the creative wellspring of living a life full of love and gratitude. She draws this inspiration from her three amazing boys, her loving and supportive husband, phenomenal family, and the beauty that surrounds her in Colorado. www.jenniferhuntdesigns.com

Dr. Matthew B. James, international trainer, lecturer, and educator, began studying spiritual disciplines at age five and trained in contemporary therapeutic techniques in his teens. He is president of Kona University and its training and seminar division, The Empowerment Partnership, where he serves as a master trainer of Neuro Linguistic Programming, a practical behavioral technology for helping people achieve their desired results in life. He has been chosen to carry on a lineage of Huna, the ancient Hawaiian science of consciousness and energy healing. Dr. James has taught many leaders in the human potential movement. His work is dedicated to creating lasting personal transformation and training people to access and use their intrinsic personal power. To learn more about Dr. James and his work, visit www.huna.com.

Jacquie Jordan is the founder of Jacquie Jordan Inc./TVGuestpert. com, a media development, production, and publishing company with the primary purpose of raising the media profile of their Guestperts while developing the self-supporting media businesses behind their brands. She is a nationally recognized and Emmy-nominated broadcast television producer. Jacquie has been featured in Entrepreneur Magazine, Selling Power Magazine, Feedback Magazine, and on the cover of Woman's World Magazine. She is a television commentator on the business of the industry and pop culture. Jacquie's appearances include Fox Reality, "Good Day New York," Fox, ABC Family, CBS, TV Guide Channel, ABC, and FX, and she can be heard and seen weekly on NewsPress Radio/KZSB 1290 AM Santa Barbara and Sony's Blip.TV. She is the author of "Get on TV! The Insider's Guide to Pitching the Producers and Promoting Yourself!" www.tvguestpert.com

Judy Kuriansky is a pioneer of radio call-in advice, and, more recently, of Internet advice. An adjunct professor at the Clinical Psychology Program at Columbia University Teachers College and visiting professor of Peking University Health Science Center in Beijing, she is a frequent commentator on international media - including CNN - on various news issues. Dr. Judy is on the advisory board of several magazines and public service organizations and works extensively in Asia on health and women's issues. Though known for her relationship advice, Dr. Judy is also an expert on emergency mental health services and has worked at Ground Zero and many other disaster sites worldwide. She also gives lectures around the world, including in the Middle East, on how to cope with world conflicts,. She is the author of numerous books, including, "How To Love A Nice Guy," "The Complete Idiot's Guide to Dating," and "Healthy Relationships." www.drjudy.com

Lori La Bey is driving change in how caregiving is perceived, received, and delivered in the world. Founder of Alzheimer's Speaks, Senior Lifestyle Trends, and Caregiver Campus, Lori is a speaker, trainer, consultant, spokesperson, and self-proclaimed, "Advocate on Steroids for Alzheimer's disease." Her mission is to shift caregiving from a "crisis-driven mode" to that of a natural evolving state as we progress through life. She can be reached through her websites, www.AlzheimersSpeaks.com and www.CaregiverCampus.com.

Manicurist-to-millionaire **Sharmen Lane** is a widely recognized four-time author, international motivational speaker, and life coach. She has been interviewed by Fox TV, "Leeza Gibbons Hollywood Confidential," Lifetime TV, Gibraltar Broadcasting Corporation TV, NPR, New York Daily News, BusinessWeek, "Coast to Coast," and many others. She has written articles for national magazines and has spoken for large companies, corporations, high schools, colleges, charities, and non-profit organizations throughout the world. As a motivational speaker, she has trained, managed, and coached thousands of individuals on what it takes to get what they want. www.sharspeaks.com

Nicole Lanning is a natural born empath, psychic intuitive, author, and healer who has focused her life on energy work, readings, and spiritual teachings. Even as a child, she knew she was different. She grew up as an early Indigo child and had a passion and love for working with her guides. Raised in a very strict, religious, God-fearing background, she has transformed her life and become a successful, Spirit-loving entrepreneur. She is the founder of Healing Art Forms Institute, Holistic Healing Minute, and the author of "Practical Crystal Healing," and she has dedicated her life to sharing her wisdom so that others may grow and learn. Based on her connection with the spirit realm, her own intuition, and practical wisdom, Nicole's readings, healings, classes, programs, books, and online video learning format have helped clients around the world learn, grow, and change. You can find out more about Nicole Lanning by visiting www.healingartforms.com and www.holistichealingminute.com.

Rick Lannoye is a social reformer, anthropology enthusiast, and religious philosopher. Time and again, he has challenged the status quo to bring society's demands on human behavior into coherence with science and reason. Recently, he's turned his attention toward the growing influence of Christian Fundamentalism, or "Pseudo Evangelicalism," and completed his second book, "Hell? No! Why You Can Be Certain There's No Such Place As Hell." www.thereisnohell.com

An innovator educated at Stanford University, the University of Pittsburgh, and Harvard Medical School, **Dr. Katharine C. McCorkle** is a psychologist with decades of experience. She developed award-winning programs for drivers under the influence of alcohol or drugs and learning-disabled delinquents and was part of the team that developed the first program for adolescent sex offenders in Pennsylvania. Dr. McCorkle is a member of the Greater Pittsburgh Psychological Association (past Chair, Continuing Education Committee), PA Psychological Association, American Psychological Association, and the Association for Comprehensive Energy Psychology. She is the founder and CEO of Balanced Heart™ Healing Center, a non-profit integrative health center for mind, body, and spirit. Balanced Heart™ Coaching, the spiritually-centered coaching program Dr. McCorkle developed, is a system of tools and strategies for living life in greater consistency with one's spiritual beliefs. Her guided journal, "A Balanced Heart: 10 Weeks to Break Through" offers readers the experience of using these tools and strategies successfully. In her faith communities, Dr. McCorkle has served on national and local boards and committees. www.balancedheart.org

Shirley W. Mitchell, known as "The Golden Egg of Aging™," is the author of six books, which include "Fabulous after 50®" and "Sensational after 60®," and is co-author of three books, including

"101 Great Ways To Improve Your Life." She is a columnist of the syndicated, "Fabulous after Fifty™" online column and featured columnist for Senior Lifestyle Magazine, Senior Evangelism Partnership, and Passionate for Life Magazine. She is also the celebrity talk show host of the syndicated radio shows "Aging Outside the Box®" and "Aging Outside the Box® Christian Spiritual Sparks™." As an aging and longevity expert, she is highly recognized as one of the top writers and speakers on aging, seniors, the Baby Boomer generation, women's issues, and healthy lifestyles. Mitchell is a member of the American Society on Aging, National Association for Female Executives, American Business Women's Association, Red Hat Society, Diva Web of Fame, and the Lit Chicks of Sand Mountain. Her online system comprises 59 websites, 13 blogs, and two dozen social sites, including Self Growth, Inc and MyExpertSolution.com. She supports the American Heart Association and the Go Red for Women Program. www.agingoutsidethebox.net

Kristen Moeller thrives while "disrupting the ordinary" and inspiring others to do the same. A highly respected coach, author, speaker, and radio show host who holds a master's degree in counseling, Kristen has more than 21 years of experience in the field of personal development. Her bestselling book, "Waiting for Jack: Confession of a Self-Help Junkie - How to Stop Waiting and Start Living Your Life," explores our pervasive human tendency to wait and look outside ourselves for answers. Jack Canfield of "Chicken Soup for the Soul" fame wrote the foreword to the book. Kristen is the creator of "Author Your Brilliance™," which empowers authors to find and express their voice, and is the executive publisher for Imbue Press. Her non-profit, the Chick-a-go Foundation, provides "pay-it-forward" scholarships for transformational educational training programs reaching people who otherwise cannot afford such opportunities. Kristen is also a celebrity ambassador to the National Eating Disorder Association. She resides in Colorado with her husband in an eco-friendly, solar-powered home. www.kristenmoeller.com

Over three decades ago, **Roy Nelson** used spiritual principles to lose 120 pounds and overcome panic attacks, phobias, and a myriad of addictions. Since then, Roy has been a spiritual mentor to a following of students from around the globe, specializing in intensive, one-on-one guidance to people who were unable to receive help through any other means. He is known as the "go-to guy" for those who cannot stop overeating or using other bad habits self-destructively. His depth of spirituality and love is so profound that often those who seek his help have their compulsions removed immediately. To learn more, visit www.RoyLovesYou.com.

Paramahamsa Nithyananda, known as the "ever-smiling swami," is a young, enlightened master of Yoga and meditation who has inspired more than four million followers worldwide. He has dedicated his life to helping people overcome mental, physical, and spiritual barriers to achieve enlightenment and live lives of bliss, success, and peace. Find out more about Nithyananda's meditation techniques and transformational processes, including the art of levitation, at www.innerawakening.org and www.dhyanapeetam.org.

Born in Nürnberg, Germany to a mystic/artist father and a musically talented mother, **Deva Premal** was taught violin and piano and received voice training. By the time she was five years old, she was already chanting the Gayatri Mantra daily and continues to integrate meditation into her life. Deva met her life and music partner Miten in India in 1990 and soon began a journey into love and creativity that has taken their inspiring blend of song, mantra, and meditation to a worldwide audience. They have released a string of acclaimed CDs, and their concerts and ecstatic chant workshops are met with rave reviews throughout Europe, Australia, South America, Canada, and the United States. Their music transcends all the usual musical boundaries, with fans including rock icon Cher, who featured one of Deva's most popular chants, the "Gayatri Mantra," on her Farewell Concert Tour; world-renowned author and motivational coach Tony Robbins, who describes their music as "passionate and powerful;" and even His Holiness The Dalai Lama, who exclaimed "Beautiful music, beautiful...!" after hearing Deva and Miten sing at a private audience. Bestselling author Eckhart Tolle notes, "As you listen to the music of Deva and Miten, the sacred space that lies beyond the mind emerges naturally and effortlessly. Pure magic." www. devapremalmiten.com

Claudio Reilsono has coached baseball for almost 30 years and is head coach at Carnegie Mellon University. He is a director of professional scouting/lead scout with Paramount Scouting Bureau and has signed over 60 players to professional contracts all over the world. Along with his coaching and scouting work, Claudio has appeared frequently on ESPN and various Pittsburgh radio and television shows. He is co-host of Pittsburgh's only television boxing show, a boxing commentator, and a professional hitting instructor. He also writes a monthly column for the Pittsburgh Sports Report, and he produced a hitting video in 2003. He conducts his own instructional camps across the country and participates in others. In 1990, as the 25-year-old head coach of Penn State Beaver, Claudio's team won a collegiate championship. He also has appeared in a movie and is a motivational speaker. Claudio dedicates his entire career to his late mother, Ida, and father, Olindo. "None of this would have happened, if it was not for their love and support." He also dedicates it to his wife, Lynda, and their 9-year-old daughter, Ida. www.claudioreilsono.com

Dea Shandera realized long ago that she is a spiritual being having a human experience. Dubbed by many as the "zen executive," she is a highly regarded and seasoned creative entertainment industry leader having served tenures over the past 25 years at Paramount Pictures, The Walt Disney Company, and MGM. Her most recent post was as executive vice president of worldwide marketing for MGM Television. Additionally, Dea has consulted in every area of the entertainment business - from publicity to production through distribution, as well as the book publishing business. She has always been a champion of stories (in books, film, and television) that celebrate the human spirit and inspire people to be their greatest yet. Some of her consulting clients: Sony Pictures Home Entertainment, Gener8Xion Entertainment, Waterside Productions, MGM, Trifecta Entertainment and Media, Rocky Mountain Pictures, The Rainbow Bridge, Spirit Rising Productions, Earth Communications Center, Off the Pier Productions, Universal Music, and authors James Redfield, William Gladstone, Jesse Dylan, Sharmen Lane, Kristen Moeller, Annie Burnside, and Peter Anthony. Dea is the proud mother of a son and daughter. In 1994, **Brent Hunter** conceived, produced, and directed the first world community in cyberspace, "The Park" (a community of 700,000+ members worldwide.) He is now recognized as the grandfather of today's modern social networking sites. In 2001, Mr. Hunter spearheaded the multi-faceted peace project titled, "The Rainbow Bridge," which bridges the gap between the old world of war, violence, and poverty to the new world reality of inner peace, world peace, reconciliation, collaboration, partnership, and harmony among all races, religions, and institutions. The second edition of his book, "The Rainbow Bridge," illuminates common ground and universal truths within the world's major religions. It has been translated into 23 languages, and a prototype board game has been created. A third edition is upcoming. Mr. Hunter has been featured in various film projects, which include, "Tapping The Source," the recent inspirational movie available on DVD from Beyond Words. brenthunter.tv

Lorelei Shellist draws from her own experiences as a runaway teen who followed her dream to travel the world and become an international model and muse. In her "not all glitz and glam" story, titled, "Runway RunAway: A Backstage Pass to Fashion, Romance & Rock 'N Roll," Lorelei writes and speaks candidly about life as a runaway, a muse to the world's top designers (YSL, Chanel's Karl Lagerfeld, Geoffrey Beene, and others,) and her struggles with her rock star fiancé's addictions until his untimely death at 30 years old. Lorelei's intrinsic connection with others has led Lorelei towards counseling women in prison, at-risk teens, and survivors of domestic abuse. With a master's degree in spiritual psychology from USM, her appeal crosses many demographics and particularly appeals to the baby boomer generation, which grew up inundated with confusing and contradictory mass media messages. Lorelei also empowers teens with her personal message, teaching them to stand up inside themselves and for themselves. She uses critical life skills and interactive exercises that motivate and inspire. www.loreleishellist. com and www.runwayrunaway.com

Dr. Joseph Shrand is an instructor of psychiatry at Harvard Medical School; the medical director of CASTLE (Clean and Sober Teens Living Empowered,) an intervention unit for at-risk teens, which is part of the highly respected High Point Treatment Center in Brockton, MA.; and an assistant child psychiatrist on the medical staff of Massachusetts General Hospital. Dr. Shrand has served as medical director of the child and adolescent outpatient program at McLean Hospital, has run several inpatient psychiatric units, and is the medical director of the Adult Inpatient Psychiatric Unit for High Point Treatment Centers in Plymouth. He is also the medical director of "Road to Responsibility," a community-based program that tends to adults with significant developmental disability. Dr. Shrand routinely gives lectures on Theory of Mind and its application to re-conceptualize the behaviors of patients. He gave a similar lecture at the 2008 annual meeting of the American Academy of Child and Adolescent Psychiatry in Chicago, to broad acclaim. Among colleagues and staff, he is affectionately called "Doctor Joe," as he was "Joe" in the original children's cast of the PBS series, "ZOOM."

Leesa Sklover, Ph.D, is a pioneer in integrative medicine and sound-music healing, a composer and performer of sacred and trans-species music, spiritual counselor, cetacean researcher, and shamanic healer. She works in A Planetree Integrative Medicine program - New Milford Hospital, in New Milford, CT. She is certified in kundalini yoga and hypnotherapy and has appeared in Vogue, New Woman, The Washington Post, Cosmo, The Discovery Channel, and Nightline. For over 20 years, she has created workshops and lectures to inspire others. Her aim is to encourage and teach exuberance and resilience in the lives she touches. She has private practice in Washington, New Milford, Ct., and NYC. She teaches at The Graduate Institute and is helping to create a global school. She is research and special projects director for Cetacean Society International, where she researches the psychoacoustics of dolphins and whales and helps lone and lost cetaceans in the wild. She worked in health and healing at Canyon Ranch Spa for 12 years and as an international consultant and teacher. Her areas of research involve the power of the creative process to heal, creative psychotherapy with the learning disabled, programs for abused children, eco-spirituality, and blended family health. She is working on a novella called, "Belugaman" and a non-fiction piece about creating a world family tree, called, "A Collection of Souls." drleesa.com and ecobluecreative.com

Cliff Snider is a husband, father, and grandfather who for the last 48 years has spent his Christmases dressed as Santa Claus. In his "real" life, he assists hundreds of artists in the production and marketing of their creative efforts. In his book, "Santa's Journey," the shadow-artist applies his own voice and hand to his creative side. Snider is the signature Santa for Christmas Castle in Jamestown, NC in an authentic 1832 medieval castle. In 2007, Cliff's story, "It Must Be Santa" was featured in "Our State" magazine, and his story of "The Praying Santa" has aired on "The 700 Club" at Christmas multiple times. In 2008, his story "The Good Book Santa" appeared in the Christmas issue of "Guideposts" magazine. He makes his home in High Point, North Carolina and can be contacted through his website at www.cliffkringle.com.

Laura Stinchfield is an internationally acclaimed pet psychic/animal communicator. She is known and respected by her colleagues and clientele for her amazingly accurate and life-changing telepathic animal communications, as well as her handling skills and knowledge of animal behavior. Laura's clientele ranges from other animal trainers (domestic and exotic,) veterinarians, rescue groups, and celebrities to private consultations with adults and children. Laura is an avid writer and columnist as well as a radio show host. Laura dedicates her life to sharing the vastness of animal consciousness. She believes that if we learn to communicate with animals more clearly, their confusion and behavior problems begin to drift away and we, in return, become more peaceful, caring people. You can read about her, watch her videos, listen to her radio shows, and reach her through her website at www.ThePetPsychic.com.

Gloria Tom Wing Staudt is an intuitive coach, personal best expert, and author of the new book, "Live Your Vacation: The Ultimate Guide to Live Your Dream Life ... Every Day!" This acclaimed guide to positive living helps people connect with their highest and best selves, achieve their dreams, and lovingly relate to others. Gloria holds a master's degree in psychology, is a certified behavioral and values analyst, and a certified money breakthrough coach with extensive experiences in private, corporate, and non-profit organizations. Through her business, Peak Success Coaching, she provides coaching, facilitation, and assessment services via telephone, Internet, and in person. Her products and services include speaking, seminars, books, retreat workshops, and transformational coaching. She is a contributing author of "Conscious Entrepreneurs - A Radical New Approach to Purpose, Passion & Profit." As an active Rotarian and past president of the Rotary Club of Burnaby Metrotown, Gloria contributes to local and global community to help create a more peaceful and loving world. For more information, visit her websites: www.PeakSuccessCoaching.com and www. LiveYourVacation.com.

Tom Von Deck is an international corporate meditation trainer, stress management speaker, and author of "Oceanic Mind - The Deeper Meditation Training Course." Through employee seminars, books, and audio courses, Tom assists people in discovering their unique routes to that place of deep inner stillness and peace within. Busy people, religious people, and nonreligious people of all walks of life discover in these programs that meditation becomes much easier when they create practices with which they are personally compatible. Tom's website is www.DeeperMeditation.Net.

Tom Wright overcame tremendous odds as he grew up in a dangerous environment overrun by the racially charged violence of the 1960s. He now looks upon these early influences as the crucible that forged his will to continually rise above his circumstances and overcome all obstacles he encounters throughout the course of his journey for a better life. A student of ancient Toltec wisdom, Ernest Holmes' work, and the martial arts, Mr. Wright is a respected Science of Mind licensed practitioner and seventh-degree black belt. Before he created "The One Penny Millionaire!™" transformational seminar, he enjoyed a long and distinguished career as a practical, personal-growth trainer; professional communicator; and writer. Early in his career, Tom Wright was a professor of English, and he served as a communications aide to two U.S. Presidents. For the latter, he was awarded a Presidential Service Citation. www. onepennymillionaire.com

About Absolute Love Publishing

Absolute Love Publishing specializes in publishing works that create love and light in the world. It is based in Austin, Texas, USA. www.absolutelovepublishing.com

About Caroline A. Shearer

Caroline A. Shearer is a bestselling author, speaker, and founder of Absolute Love Publishing. Her well-regarded books include the "Adventures of a Lightworker" mystery series. Known as a fresh, distinctive spiritual voice, Caroline's vision is to promote goodness in the world through the inspiration of others.

11920050R00134

Made in the USA
Charleston, SC
29 March 2012